FACULTY PRODUCTIVITY

GARLAND STUDIES IN HIGHER EDUCATION
VOLUME 15
GARLAND REFERENCE LIBRARY OF SOCIAL SCIENCE
VOLUME 1396

FACULTY PRODUCTIVITY
FACTS, FICTIONS, AND ISSUES

EDITED BY
WILLIAM G. TIERNEY

FALMER PRESS
A MEMBER OF THE TAYLOR & FRANCIS GROUP
NEW YORK AND LONDON
1999

Library of Congress Cataloging-in-Publication Data

Faculty productivity : facts, fictions, and issues / by William G. Tierney.

        p.   cm. — (Garland studies in higher education ; vol. 15. Garland reference library of social science ; vol. 1396.)

    Includes bibliographical references and index (p. 183).

    ISBN 0-8153-3220-3 (alk. paper)

    1. Sex—Reference books.   2. Reference books—Sex.   3. Sex—Library resources.   I. Title.   II. Garland reference library of social science ; v. 1396.

Z7164.S42L55   1999

869'.3—dc20   93-37236

                                                           CIP

Printed on acid-free, 250-year-life paper

Manufactured in the United States of America

Contents

Acknowledgments

Much of the work for this book has been sponsored by the Pew Charitable Trusts. The opinions expressed are those of the authors and do not necessarily reflect the views of The Pew Charitable Trusts.

Series Editor's Preface

Higher education is a multifaceted phenomenon in modern society, combining a variety of institutions and an increasing diversity of students, a range of purposes and functions, and different orientations. The series combines research-based monographs, analyses, and discussions of broader issues and reference books related to all aspects of higher education. It is concerned with policy as well as practice from a global perspective. The series is dedicated to illuminating the reality of higher and postsecondary education in contemporary society.

Philip G. Altbach
Boston College

Rethinking Faculty Work
Challenges and Possibilities

William G. Tierney
University of Southern California

Academic life at the beginning of the twenty-first century will be incomparably different from what took place on college campuses as the nineteenth century ended. Such a statement seems matter-of-fact and obvious. Nonetheless it is important to stress. A common perception is that colleges and universities do not change, that faculty are wedded to the status quo, that administrators are incapable of implementing innovations, and that reform in areas such as curricula is all but impossible. It is easier to move a graveyard, I have heard it said, than to get a faculty to agree on anything.

Yet, as with other social organizations in the United States, colleges and universities have undergone a sea change in personnel, function, structure, and purpose during the last one hundred years. At the turn of the twentieth century, the administrative structure was thin—a president and perhaps a dean or two—and the faculty often did not hold doctorates. Some of the largest and fastest growing sectors currently at play in academia—community colleges, proprietary institutions, for-profit and corporate universities—did not even exist in the manner akin to what they are today. Research was sporadic at best, and not preeminent. Faculty could be fired at will, and ideas such as academic freedom did not provide any substantial meaning for the vast majority of faculty and administrators. Fund-raising did not consume a president's time in the way it does today, and alliances with business and industry or local communities were nothing comparable to what they have become. And of course, technological changes such as electronic mail, faxes, and a host of scientific advances have changed the nature of faculty work. Postsecondary education has become a $250 billion—dollar industry.

My point here simply is not to speak with pride or dismay about all of these changes but to argue that rather than remain static, colleges and universities have been remarkably dynamic institutions. True, anyone who sits on a faculty committee will bemoan the deliberate, some will say lethargic, pace of decision making. But we need do no more than consider the revolutionary changes that have taken place in this century to underscore my point about the dynamism that exists in academe.

The impetus for change has come, in general, from three directions. First, the needs and leadership of participants in the academic enterprise often have directed change: Tenure codes are one example of a reform which those within the institution demanded. Second, postsecondary institutions also have responded to the demands of external constituencies and environments. The elaboration of student services in large part reflects the array of needs of the consumers; scientific research often came about because federal or state governments provided funds and tried to direct action in a particular area. And third, advances in society also impacted on collegiate life. E-mail has made collaboration with one's colleagues a continent away commonplace; air travel has enabled many parents to send their children to college's thousands of miles away from home.

Thus, as we look to the next century, we ought not to presume that colleges and universities will appear tomorrow as they are today. Changes from within academe will still take place; external constituencies will have needs; society at large will change. Peter Drucker, the respected management theorist, garnered much publicity when he observed that colleges and universities will look quite different not in one hundred years, but in a generation. His trenchant comment was that change will be so dramatic that "universities won't survive" (Duderstadt, 1997, p. 1). I tend to agree that significant changes will take place within a short time period, but I am not so quick to predict academe's demise. The pressures for change are largely five: (1) money, (2) prestige, (3) the organization of academic work, (4) governance structure, and (5) purpose.

MONEY

There may be a variety of different, or more delicate, ways to define the problem, but the long and short is that colleges and universities in the future will receive reduced revenue streams from the federal and state governments. As Daniel Layzell outlines in chapter 1, even in recent years when state appropriations have increased ever so slightly they are not close to what we received a decade ago. The federal government, for its part, seems less inclined to play a significant role in academic life. As James Duderstadt (1997) has observed, "the relationship [had] been one that would be best described as a partnership, particularly in the area of research. Today that partnership has unraveled. It has become more a process of procurement than a partnership" (p. 3). The need for additional fiscal resources will only increase.

PRESTIGE

The broad citizenry has lost the respect it once had for those involved in academe. The popular jeremiads that invoke disdain for faculty and administrative life may be one source to blame; it is in vogue today to lob attacks and paint caricatures of academics. Oftentimes the responses to such criticism are encoded in academic jargon that does not translate well to the general public. Academics frequently come off as uncaring or intellectual snobs. However, academe's problem today is more than simply the need for a good public relations firm to deal with the Charles Sykeses and William Bennetts of the world.

Rather, the public needs to have a better sense of what the purpose of academic life should be, and how college and university leaders go about meeting that mission. Too often, faculty appear disengaged from the so-called real world in a way that does not invoke images of a dispassionate search for truth; instead faculty appear desirous of doing whatever they please, and the public be dammed. Thus, the need for clearer definitions of academic work will surely increase.

THE ORGANIZATION OF ACADEMIC WORK

One area that actually has not seen too much change during the twentieth century is how we organize classes and teach them. In general, students take a "class" for a specific period of time—usually a semester or a quarter—for a set number of hours each week. The lecture is still the preferred form of delivery. Two external changes will force the majority of colleges and universities to alter such a leisurely pedagogical pace. Technology—e-mail, web-sites, distance learning—enable faculty to teach in ways that no one could have envisioned only a generation ago. Increasingly, many students also no longer desire gaps of time—summer vacations and the like—between their learning experiences, and/or they need part-time coursework or intensive learning experiences. Such technological abilities and consumer preferences will force colleges and universities to rethink the delivery of educational programming—or face Drucker's prediction.

GOVERNANCE STRUCTURE

We often forget that at the outset of the twentieth century, faculty participation in governance was by and large nonexistent or minimal. Organizational structure was thin. The vast majority of decision-making structures—if one can call a president and three administrators a governance structure—made decisions without much faculty input. Today postsecondary institutions have the remnants of a "shared governance" structure that virtually everyone agrees is not working very well. Administrators decry the inability to get decisions made, and faculty are equally unhappy with the power and authority that has been assumed by boards of trustees, presidents, and senior administrators.

My purpose here is not to offer an exegesis on how we have arrived at a governance system that seems in need of repair, and an organizational structure that may well befit standard organizations of twenty years ago but not today. One can find any number of well-reasoned treatises about why postsecondary institutions have evolved in the ways they have and how the organization might change (Tierney, 1998a, 1998b). However, in an age that many define as postmodern, such rigid structures and dysfunctional decision-making systems demand redefinition and reform. The point is neither to say that there should be greater or less faculty voice, nor that a specific organizational structure should be eliminated or reshaped. Instead, I am suggesting that structures always change; rather than assume rigidity and the status quo, we must develop forms that fit more clearly the needs of the future rather than the past.

PURPOSE

The first four points that I have raised—money, prestige, academic work, and governance structures—all bespeak to this final overarching issue. What society expects of colleges and universities today is dramatically different from what was desired a century ago, and even a generation ago. No one could have predicted in 1900 that research would play such a fundamental role in academic life. No one would have predicted in 1970 that for-profit universities such as the University of Phoenix would experience the growth, and receive the degree of academic legitimacy, that they have. There appears to be a vital need to define what individual institutions and faculties should be doing. It is easy to suggest that faculty need to have a greater engagement with society, but what specifically that engagement is, what form it takes, and how it alters academic life remain to be worked out. Again, if those involved in academe avoid the issue of organizational purpose and design, they run the risk of working in institutions that are antiquated and serve no useful purpose. Other entities will arise to serve the needs of the external environment. But since academe's participants always have responded to such needs by changing in one way or another, I am confident that we will meet these new challenges as well.

To meet these challenges depends in large part on the will of the faculty and the decisions the professorate makes about the nature of professorial life. What should faculty be doing? How do we know if faculty are performing effectively or are merely well-paid laggards? At a time when industry has dramatically reshaped its workforce and become more productive, why do faculty seem out of touch and incapable of reform? In one way or another, if colleges and universities are to deal effectively with the problems listed above, then they must deal with the work of the faculty. Some will say that academe's money problems exist because so much of an institution's income is taken up by salaries due to tenure. Others will suggest that faculty have low prestige in the eyes of the citizenry because they are unproductive. Organizational reform in one way or another has to deal with faculty roles within the organization in the same way that the purpose of the organization needs to come to grips with what the role of the faculty is and what it should be. Is a productive faculty member one who teaches to the exclusion of research? Should work in the community be encouraged? Should a college or university continue to evaluate teaching in the way that is currently done, or is it advisable to develop alternative criteria?

All of these issues turn on the idea of productivity. The goal of this book is to offer a variety of ways one might think about the nature of faculty work. Any organization ought not to change merely for the sake of change. And colleges and universities ought not to move in one direction if individuals do not have tightly reasoned arguments and data to support a particular reform. Thus, instead of a unified proposal where all chapters' authors agree with one another, in this book I have purposely assembled a diverse group of texts where ideas at times conflict and at other times complement one another. All of the chapters are informative about a topic that is controversial to some and preeminent to others. My hope is that after reading this book the authors' ideas will have generated more light than heat about how colleges and universities might change or retain particular aspects of faculty roles and rewards.

In chapter 1 Daniel Layzell expands on the contexts in which academe finds itself, and then proffers traditional concepts of productivity based on econometric and business models. He points out how faculty work is typically at odds with standard productivity measurements because of the autonomous and asynchronous nature of academic life. He makes an artful case for why academe needs to change and highlights how one might reconceptualize academic inputs and outputs by focusing on organizational processes. He concludes by considering the roles of different constituencies such as the federal and state governments and the various actors within the organization.

In chapter 2 I extend Layzell's analysis of productivity, but in a specific direction. I point out that the terms that economists use when they write about productivity are frequently jarring and alien to how faculty think about their work. My concern is not so much to convince faculty to use a word—productivity—but rather to reform academic work. Accordingly, I employ an anthropological notion of productivity that John Collier first used when he worked with Native Americans. Rather than a production line mentality that incorporates inputs and outputs, I suggest that faculty and administrators work from notions of organizational culture and develop ways to enable people to be productive.

Productivity demands that individuals think of the needs of the community and how the collective is able to help the individual, and vice versa, how the individual is best able to contribute to the collective. I elaborate on the idea of performance contracts as one way to enable individuals to contribute to the culture in ways that accentuate their strengths. As Diamond and Adam point out in chapter 4, such a framework moves away from a production line mentality where everyone needs to do the same work and those who perform best at the same work are perceived to be the most productive. Instead, multiple activities are rewarded.

However much Layzell and I might suggest ways to improve the organizational workplace, the world will not change tomorrow and an organization's participants need ways to assess how individuals perform today. Chapters 3 and 4 take up these challenges. James Fairweather considers in chapter 3 what accounts for a highly productive faculty member. In particular he considers two overarching issues: (1) how productive faculty are in teaching and research, and (2) whether it is possible for individuals to be productive simultaneously in research, teaching, and service.

By way of careful analysis of the *National Survey of Post-secondary Faculty (NSOPF),* Fairweather considers those factors that affect productivity. He highlights how issues such as institutional type play a fundamental role in how individuals perceive productivity and are able to be productive. He points out how difficult it is for an individual to be good at all tasks, and offers the idea that perhaps what is necessary is that a department be able to have a standard concept of departmental excellence for which all individuals contribute differently and yet are rewarded similarly.

Robert Diamond and Bronwyn Adam in chapter 4 extend Fairweather's point by turning their attention to how one might document diversity. Over the last decade many disciplinary associations have developed statements that expand traditional notions of scholarship. Diamond and Adam accept these ideas and consider how one might operationalize them. Their goal is to do for a panoply of scholarly activities what has been done for the evaluation of research. That is, over the last generation the professorate has done a relatively good job of assessing a faculty member's research. When someone comes up for tenure there are multiple criteria used to evaluate the individual's research. If a college or university expands the definition of what counts for productivity, however, then the institution needs as rigorous standards about what constitutes "good work" in any number of other areas. Simply because an individual works in schools, for example, is insufficient evidence that he or she is excellent at that task. How, then, might a review committee at an institution accurately evaluate someone's work?

Thus, chapter 4 considers what might go into a "professional portfolio" that enables the full range of activities to be documented and evaluated. The portfolio that Diamond and Adam discuss has a close linkage to the kinds of suggestions made in chapter 2. If an institution were to accept that a performance contract needs to be instituted, then the logical next step would be a decision about what constitutes a professional portfolio.

In chapter 5 James Hearn turns the idea of productivity on its head and considers how salaries function to reward productive members in research universities. After a historical overview of faculty salary structures, Hearn considers a wealth of factors (e.g., inflation, professional fields) that impact on how salaries are constructed. He then goes on to point out the tenuous nature of salary structures and faculty performance and considers how institutions often violate principles of productivity with regard to who gets paid the most, or how much one person's salary versus another's. His analysis is provocative, compelling, and convincing. The reader comes away from the chapter more convinced that change is needed. Hearn then turns to a variety of policy options that one might employ to bring greater equity into the system, not so that everyone's salary would be equal, but that a more just system might be developed.

Yvonna Lincoln concludes the book by offering in chapter 6 a synthesis of the chapters and suggesting additional avenues that need to be explored, expanded, or conjoined. In particular, she argues that there are certain aspects of faculty work that cannot be measured upon a productivity index. She also points to the need for greater discussion about academic freedom, and argues that conversations about faculty productivity that neglect its connection to the professorate's search for truth are mistaken.

My aim here is for the reader to finish these texts with a better understanding of how productivity has been construed and how it might be reshaped. Armed with such information, those of us concerned with changing the academic enterprise are better able to overcome the problems and challenges that confront colleges and universities.

REFERENCES

Duderstadt, James. (1997). "Revolutionary changes: Understanding the challenges and the possibilities." *Business Officer* (July); 1–15.

Tierney, William G. (1998a). *The responsive university: Restructuring for high performance.* Baltimore, MD: Johns Hopkins University Press.

———. (1998b).

FACULTY PRODUCTIVITY

Higher Education's Changing Environment

Faculty Productivity and the Reward Structure

Daniel T. Layzell
Principal, MGT of America, Inc.

INTRODUCTION

This chapter will address the concepts of faculty productivity and the faculty reward structure within the context of the economic, political, demographic, educational, and technological transformations that are shaping higher education for the next century. Many researchers and policy analysts (e.g., Mingle, 1996; Layzell, Lovell, and Gill, 1996) have argued that the ongoing public concerns regarding faculty productivity are related in part to the fact that existing faculty reward structures are not in sync with the public's main goals for higher education (i.e., undergraduate education and service). Instead, faculty reward structures appear to be heavily geared toward research and scholarship. This disjuncture has led to several initiatives to "fix the problem," including legislation, accountability reporting, mandated workload policies, and post-tenure review.

The purpose of this chapter is to explore the fundamental ways in which higher education's climate is changing and how the current conceptions and policy frameworks underlying both faculty productivity and faculty rewards are inadequate to meet the needs of institutions of higher education and their stakeholders as they enter a new era. It should be noted at the outset that the primary focus of this chapter is on public higher education, although many of the trends and issues to be discussed affect private higher education as well and are also mentioned where appropriate. The chapter will describe the trends and transformations shaping higher education; evaluate the fit between where higher education is heading and the current conceptions of faculty productivity and faculty rewards; provide a new organizing principle to meet these challenges; and discuss the role of the federal government, state governments, and institutions in helping to position higher education for the challenges of the future.

THE CURRENT CONTEXT SHAPING HIGHER EDUCATION

There are many external and internal factors and forces shaping the current context for higher education. These factors and forces can be broadly grouped into the following categories: economic, political, demographic, and educational/technological. This section will evaluate how these forces are currently impacting colleges and universities and what this might mean for the future.

Economic Context

The economic condition of higher education is directly related to the condition of its funding sources. Institutions of higher education have three primary sources of income: state governments, federal government, and tuition and fees. Each will be discussed in turn.

State Funding for Higher Education

Other than the funding provided for K-12 education, few parts of state general fund budgets have been as large as the allocation for higher education. According to the Center for Higher Education at Illinois State University, states appropriated a total of $46.5 billion in FY 1997, up 5 percent from FY 1996.

Higher education accounted for 11.5 percent of state general fund budgets in FY 1997, according to the most recent survey of state budget actions by the National Conference of State Legislatures. This is up from FY 1996 levels (11 percent) but down from FY 1988, when higher education accounted for 14.6 percent of state general fund budgets (see Figure 1.1).

Distributional changes within state budgets are largely a zero-sum game, and much of higher education's decline as a proportion of state general fund budgets in recent years may be attributed to the rapid growth in state funds appropriated for Medicaid and corrections. In FY 1991, Medicaid represented 10.1 percent of total state general fund spending (higher education was at 13.5 percent). By FY 1994, this proportion had jumped to 13.6 percent (higher education was at 12 percent). The sources of Medicaid growth include growth in health care unit costs, increased caseloads, and federal mandates expanding the scope and breadth of Medicaid coverage. The non discretionary aspect of Medicaid has a significant impact on the funds available for higher education and other discretionary areas of state budgets, especially in the tight fiscal environments of late.

Figure 1.1. Higher education's share of state general fund budgets
(From National Conference of State Legislatures, various years.)

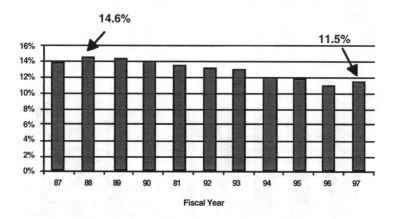

In FY 1997, the largest percent increase of all areas of state spending was for corrections (i.e., prisons) at 6.2 percent, although corrections spending represents slightly more than half of that for higher education. The significant increase in prison-related spending reflects in part current public attitudes and concerns about crime and criminals, and this area may be the next big contender for state funds. As an example, an analysis of California's "three strikes" legislation (i.e., significantly increased mandatory prison time for repeat felony offenders) suggests that such laws could seriously limit state funding for other public services in the future—not the least of which is higher education (California Higher Education Policy Center, 1994).

State appropriations for public colleges and universities constitute the major portion of state higher education appropriations. In the same vein, state appropriations constitute a significant portion of funding for the operations of public colleges and universities. Some states also make direct appropriations or payments to private institutions although the amounts are but a fraction of the state support provided to public institutions.

Figure 1.2 shows the trend in state appropriations as a percentage of current funds revenue between FY 1986 and FY 1994 for public institutions. As illustrated, this proportion declined steadily over time to approximately 33 percent in FY 1994. As a point of comparison, for private institutions this proportion declined from 0.9 percent to 0.4 percent during this same period.

Figure 1.2 State appropriations as a share of all public institution revenue

(From National Center for Educational Statistics, 1996.)

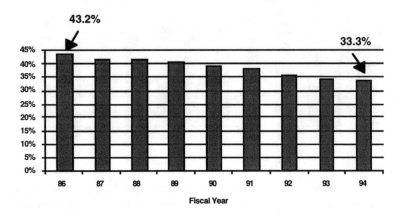

Federal Support to Higher Education.

The federal government provides support for higher education in two primary ways: student financial aid, and research and development funding. The purposes of each funding stream are different. Support for student aid is provided to promote equal access for individuals from all income levels to postsecondary education, while support for research and development is provided to encourage basic and applied research in areas of national interest (e.g., health, basic science, defense). Trends in each area are described in the following sections.

FEDERAL SUPPORT OF STUDENT FINANCIAL AID. The federal government is the largest source of all student financial aid—75 percent of the total in 1994–95 (College Board, 1995). Total federally supported student aid grew from $15.2 billion in 1984–85 to $35.1 billion in 1994–95, a change of 131 percent, outpacing inflation. However, the growth in major aid categories during this period varied significantly. Total funding for federally supported grant programs grew from $3.5 billion to $6.3 billion, a change of 80 percent. The largest of these grant programs, Pell Grants, grew from $3.0 billion to $5.6 billion, a change of 86 percent. Grants declined from 23 percent to 18 percent as a proportion of all federal aid during this period. Total funding for federally supported student loan programs grew from $9.3 billion to $25.6 billion, a change of 176 percent. Guaranteed loan programs (i.e., Stafford, PLUS, SLS) remained the single largest group of programs at $24.7 billion. Loans grew from 61 percent to 73 percent as a proportion of all federal aid during this period. Total funding for the federal college work-study program grew from $645 million to $749 million, a change of 18 percent. This program accounted for 2 percent of all federal aid in 1994–95, down from 12 percent in 1984–85. In short, while the growth in federally supported student aid grew at a more rapid rate than inflation during this period, there has been a definite shift toward the use of loans for student financial aid purposes at the federal level over the past several years.

FEDERAL SUPPORT FOR RESEARCH AND DEVELOPMENT (R&D). As with student aid, the federal government is the largest single source of funding for academic R&D expenditures, representing 60 percent of the total in FY 1993 (National Science Foundation, 1995). The federal government provides funding for academic R&D via two methods: through granting agencies (e.g., Department of Defense, National Science Foundation) and through direct appropriations for earmarked projects. Estimated federal spending for academic R&D in FY 1996 totaled $15.7 billion, an increase of 38.9 percent since FY 1988, outpacing inflation (National Center for Education Statistics, 1996).

Trends in Tuition and Fees.

Tuition and fees at both public and private institutions have grown at about double the rate of inflation the past 15 years (Hauptman, 1997). Not surprisingly, as indicated in Figure 1.3, both public and private institutions have become more reliant on this revenue source to fund their operating costs.

Public institutions now derive almost one-fifth of their total revenues from tuition and fees, while private institutions get more than two-fifths. The reasons for the increased reliance on tuition and fee revenues vary between the two sectors. For public institutions, this trend is largely due to the need to make up the gap left by shortfalls in state tax support discussed earlier in this chapter. For private institutions, who are already highly dependent on tuition and fees to finance their operations, increases in tuition are related to costs of production (e.g., faculty, staff), outpacing inflation (Hauptman, 1997).

Figure 1.3 Tuition and fees as a percentage of all institutional revenue

(From National Center for Education Statistics, 1996.)

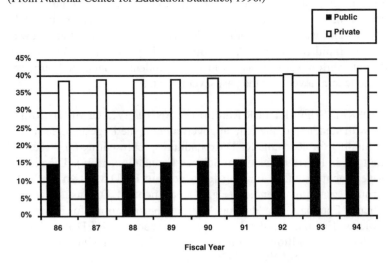

Fiscal Year

Political Context

There are three main political trends currently impacting higher education, and public higher education in particular: an increased desire from its external publics for accountability; concerns about the affordability of a college education; and an interest in linking funding to institutional performance.

At its broadest level, accountability refers to the responsibility of higher education to report on its failures and achievements to its external stakeholders within a set of mutually agreed-upon goals and objectives. The concept of public higher education being accountable to external agencies has been in place for several decades. Since the 1960s, however, the focus of accountability has shifted from a fiduciary orientation to an orientation focused on outcomes and performance. This is not to suggest that state or federal governments have abandoned interest in financial control systems, but that they have become increasingly interested in the *return on investment*. The questions now being asked by state policymakers have gone beyond merely "Were the dollars spent appropriately?" to also consider "What did we achieve with the dollars spent?" Accountability itself has become an umbrella for a variety of issues, such as the quality of, and access to, undergraduate education, affordability, and administrative costs. While the laundry list of issues varies from state to state, the common thread running throughout is an increased emphasis on quality, outcomes, and product, primarily in the area of undergraduate instruction.

The second area relates to concerns about the affordability of higher education for current and future students. Policymakers have linked increasing college costs to higher education's inability to manage institutional spending efficiently, which ultimately leads to questions about faculty productivity. The rapid growth in tuition and fees mentioned earlier has led to concerns about the affordability of higher education. A 1992 survey of State Higher Education Executive Officers (SHEEOs) and system heads found that concerns about the shifting balance between state funding and tuition revenues, and the potentially adverse impact on access to higher education, were second only to concerns about the adequacy of state financial support (Russell, 1992). Externally, state policymakers, the media, and the public at large have been critical of tuition increases within the overall context of concerns about institutional cost increases and maintaining access to higher education for state residents.

The third trend—linking funding to institutional performance—grows out of the increased interest in accountability mentioned previously. Performance-based funding is the logical extension of policymaker interest in accountability, and it directly ties together accountability, performance, and funding levels. Performance or incentive funding initiatives for higher education have had some success, most notably in Tennessee (Folger, 1989). Tennessee's incentive funding program and the additional funding received by institutions both directly and indirectly as the result of this program have been held up as the prime example of gaining public support by documenting performance.

A recent survey found that at least 11 states had performance funding programs for higher education either in place or in the process of implementation (Layzell and Caruthers, 1995). Several other states were considering the adoption of such programs, and of special note is the performance funding program for higher education enacted by the legislature in South Carolina and now being implemented by the South Carolina Commission on Higher Education. This program is based on institutional performance across 37 specific performance indicators which will be phased in through the year 2000. At that point *100 percent* of state funding for public higher education will be allocated based on institutional performance in these indicators.

Demographic Context

The demographic picture of higher education has changed over the past several years both for students and faculty. A much larger proportion of students now enrolled in higher education are outside of the traditional age population of college students than in the past. In fall 1994, 44 percent of all students enrolled were age 25 or older compared with 28 percent in fall 1970 (NCES, 1996). A not unrelated trend is the increased number of part-time students enrolled now versus in the past. In fall 1994, 43 percent of all students were enrolled on a part-time basis compared with 32 percent in fall 1970. The number of age 25 and older students is projected to continue to increase to the year 2000, and then decrease slightly, representing 40 percent of the total by fall 2006. The number of part-timers is projected to grow through fall 2006, but will represent a slightly lower proportion of the total at that point—39 percent (NCES, 1996).

For faculty, there are no trend data available on a national level regarding trends in the age distribution of faculty, although there are institutional- and system-level data documenting the "aging" of the faculty. For example, a recent University of Wisconsin System (UW System) study found that the proportion of tenured and tenure-track faculty age 55 and older within the system increased from 27 percent to 32 percent between 1985–86 and 1994–95, while the proportion age 40 and under decreased from 22 percent to 16 percent during this same period (UW System, 1996a). On a national level, one-third (32.8 percent) of all instructional faculty were age 50 or older in fall 1992 with another 18 percent age 45 to 49 (NCES, 1996). Assuming that there have been no shifts in the age distribution between then and now, this means that half of all instructional faculty in the United States could now be at or very near retirement age.

Perhaps a more important trend with regard to the subject of faculty work and productivity is the increased trend toward using part-time faculty to provide instruction. As indicated in Figure 1.4, the proportion of instructional faculty nationally on part-time contracts increased from 22 percent in fall 1970 to 40 percent in fall 1993. Of note is the significant upswing in recent years. This may be a result of the recession in the early 1990s that also had negative impacts on the finances of colleges and universities. Institutions seeking budgetary flexibility in response to fiscal downturns have more of an incentive to meet short-term instructional needs via part-time instructional staff. However, the longer-term increase in the proportion of part-time faculty may also be reflective of an overall trend on campuses to increase their staffing flexibility.

Educational/Technological Context

There are two primary, and somewhat interrelated, educational and technological shifts affecting higher education today. The first is the growing movement toward the use of distance learning and other instructional technologies to supplement, or in some cases replace, on-campus learning. The second shift is the increasing number of competitors entering the higher education marketplace in order to meet the needs of working adults and other place-bound learners. While these trends may not have the apparent urgency as the economic and political trends discussed earlier, both are likely to be as important in shaping higher education's future operating environment.

Figure 1.4 Proportion of total instructional faculty that are part-time, fall 1970 to fall 1993

(From National Center for Education Statistics, 1996, Table 220. Data for 1988, 1990, and 1992 not provided.)

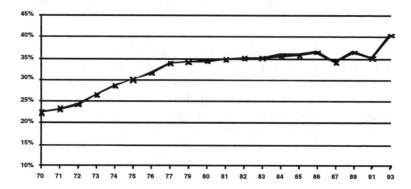

Distance Learning and Instructional Technologies

The underlying concept of distance learning—allowing place- or time-bound students to take courses or progress toward a degree without having to come to campus—has been around for several decades in the form of correspondence courses and other off-campus instructional offerings. The advent of televised instructional offerings and universities without walls in the 1960s and 1970s added yet another wrinkle to this concept. For the most part, however, this has been a secondary part of the instructional offerings of most colleges and universities.

Today, many institutions, systems, and states are beginning to consider the use of distance learning and other instructional technologies in much more fundamental ways than ever before. This can be attributed to at least three factors.

- The development of newer telecommunications technologies (i.e., fiber-optic networks)
- The rapid growth in Internet usage and supporting technologies
- The desire to broaden access to postsecondary offerings for individuals and organizations without having to build new campuses or expand existing institutions

The Western Governors University currently being developed in the western United States provides an instructive example of this trend. This initiative of the Western Governors' Association seeks to expand opportunities to participate in higher education for residents in the western United States via distance learning technologies (Zuniga, forthcoming). It will "bundle" courses and program offerings from a variety of institutions and states through a central clearinghouse and registration point.

Two issues that bear directly on the future success (or failure) of distance learning and instructional technology usage are incentives for faculty participation and ongoing faculty development activities. Institutions that want to move into this area will need to provide incentives for faculty participation such as release time and technical support. Perhaps more important, institutions will have to provide ongoing training and development opportunities to faculty who are utilizing these technologies in order to maximize their effective usage.

New Competitors: Corporate and Proprietary Institutions

Traditional colleges and universities have largely had a monopoly on the provision of higher education in the United States in this century. Because of this, higher education has been a producer-dominated enterprise whereby the faculty and institutional administration have had virtual control over the what, how, where, and when of instructional delivery. The consumers (i.e., students, parents, taxpayers) have largely been passive participants (Finn, 1997).

There are some indications that the marketplace for higher education services is entering a new era of competition as we approach the year 2000. The advent of distance learning and other instructional technologies discussed previously is ushering in a number of potential for-profit competitors such as Microsoft and IBM who are seeking to leverage their existing technological niche in higher education into a full-service educational operation. The most vivid example of this might be the University of Phoenix, which now enrolls thousands of individuals in its programs and offers complete degree programs online.

It is not clear that traditional institutions of higher education have realized this competitive threat. As indicated in a recent essay (Policy Perspectives, 1996):

Unfettered by the traditions of the academy, these specialized
providers have understood the growing demand for higher education
to address interests and needs that evolve throughout life; and they
are proving that they can provide educational programs to satisfy a
consumer movement increasingly concerned with attaining the
credential that programs of postsecondary education are expected to
provide (p. 3).

These providers have seen the great potential in meeting the needs of
older, working individuals who would like to return to college to obtain
the credentials necessary to progress in their career but who only have
limited time available (i.e., the growth in the older, part-time student
body shown earlier). In short, these providers have begun shifting the
paradigm from a producer to a consumer-dominated industry (Mingle,
1996). This shift may be hastened by the trend discussed earlier toward
more of the cost of higher education being borne by the consumer (i.e.,
students) either directly through tuition and fees or ultimately through
student loan repayment.

Summary of Trends

In summary, higher education's changing environment can be described
as follows:

* Stagnating state support and an increased reliance on tuition and
  fees to finance institutional operating costs
* Increased reliance on student loans in student aid policy
* Increased desire for accountability and linking funding to
  institutional performance by external stakeholders
* The advent of instructional technology and distance learning and
  rising competition from nontraditional providers

These trends form the context for higher education's movement into the
twenty-first century and the way in which faculty productivity and
faculty rewards will be viewed.

THE CURRENT SITUATION: CONCEPTIONS OF FACULTY WORK, REWARDS, AND PRODUCTIVITY

This section will shift from the macro-level trends affecting the future of higher education to examine how the issues of faculty work, rewards, and productivity are currently conceived.

The Content of Faculty Work

The content of faculty work is distinguished by its mode of production and distinctive attributes. Faculty work is comprised of instruction, research, and service activities. At its most basic level, though, all faculty work involves the transfer, discovery, and application of knowledge. This is not unique from other knowledge-based professions, but there are three factors in particular that distinguish the production and content of faculty work.

- *A high level of autonomy in the production process.* Faculty are trained to work independently beginning with their immersion in the culture of graduate school. This carries forward into their professional lives, where faculty are highly autonomous professionals who have significant freedom over the mode of production in their instruction, research, and service activities. A corollary to this is the fact that the working relationship between faculty and their "customers" (e.g., students) is not as direct as in other professions (lack of feedback and evaluation).
- *Asynchronous production.* Most faculty do not work the typical 9 to 5 schedule that many other professions have. Outside of regularly scheduled courses, faculty work can and does happen at any time. The advent of such technologies as e-mail and the Internet have made this even more so, whereby faculty can advise students, correspond with colleagues, or conduct research at any time of day or night. This is also one of the least understood aspects of faculty work for many nonacademics, calling into question the rigor of faculty work and productivity for these individuals.
- *The preeminence of the discipline in faculty work life.* This is perhaps best illustrated at major research universities where loyalty to the institution or even to the school/college is clearly secondary to loyalty to the discipline and its values and mores in determining faculty priorities and behaviors in the workplace. This is contrary

to the culture of most other professional fields (with perhaps the exception of medicine-although that may be changing with the rapid spread of HMOs and other managed care plans), where professionals are encouraged to conform to the values and traditions of the organization by which they are employed.

Faculty Rewards

It should be stated at the outset that the vaguely Pavlovian term faculty rewards is inherently subjective. This is because each individual faculty member resonates to a different set of incentives as he or she goes about his or her work. For the purposes of discussion, though, faculty rewards will be separated into two primary areas: compensation, and promotion and tenure.

Faculty Compensation

Staff compensation is the single largest expense for most institutions of higher education, and faculty compensation is typically the largest out-lay. Figure 1.5 shows the trend in average faculty salaries between 1984–85 and 1994–95 for public four-year, public two-year, and private institutions in constant 1994–95 dollars. As indicated, average faculty salaries grew at rates faster than inflation through the latter part of the 1980s. Salaries at public institutions have remained relatively flat throughout the 1990s, while salaries at private institutions have grown slightly in inflation-adjusted terms.

Promotion and Tenure

While the focus of this chapter is productivity, tenure is such an integral part of the faculty reward structure that it should be briefly mentioned here. The proportion of all tenured faculty in institutions of higher education has remained relatively stable since 1980 at 61 to 65 percent (NCES, 1996). Figure 1.6 shows the proportion of tenured full-time instructional faculty by institutional type for selected years between 1980–81 and 1994–95. As indicated, the proportion of tenured full-time instructional faculty has remained relatively stable within each sector during this period. However, these data belie the recent public debates regarding tenure. Beginning with the very public discussion of tenure at the University of Minnesota in 1996, the cyclical, and emotional, debate whether tenure is "sinecure" or the integral component of the preservation of academic freedom has fired up again both outside and inside the academy.

Figure 1.5 Average salary of full-time instructional faculty, in constant 1994–95 dollars

(From National Center for Education Statistics, 1996, Table 229.)

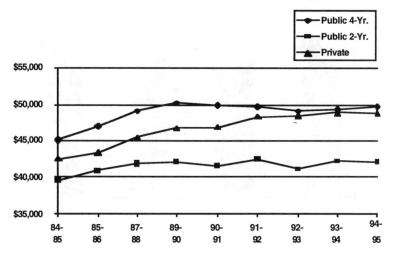

The public has a difficult time understanding why it is subject to layoff or termination while its neighbor the tenured faculty member never has to worry about such things. Trustees, presidents, and other institutional managers argue that tenure is one of the single greatest impediments to managerial flexibility by preventing them from addressing the rapidly changing fiscal/economic climate in a timely and effective manner. Some will also say that tenure keeps the deadwood ensconced in academic departments, further reducing the productivity of the institution. On the other hand, the faculty argue vociferously for the preservation of tenure to preserve academic freedom and as protection against arbitrary and capricious behavior on the part of management. While these are certainly examples of attitudes at the extreme, the intensity of the debate this time around suggests that there may be serious proposals from both sides for change to the current tenure system.

Figure 1.6 Proportion of tenured full-time instructional faculty, by type of institution, Selected years

(From National Center for Education Statistics, 1996, Table 235.)

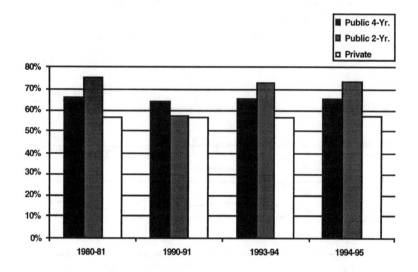

Measuring Faculty Productivity: Perennial Issues and Indices

Perennial Issues in Measuring Faculty Productivity

At the broadest level, *productivity* refers to the way in which a firm transforms inputs (e.g., labor and capital) into outputs (Hopkins, 1990). In industrial settings, productivity is relatively easy to define and measure. One need only take a selected output for a firm and divide by the input of choice (e.g., per worker). Colleges and universities, however, are not steel mills or auto plants. While some inputs are quantifiable (e.g., number of students, faculty time), "outcomes are diffuse, and difficult to measure" in higher education (Mingle and Lenth, 1989, p. 13).

There are various reasons why the definition and measurement of productivity in higher education is so vexing.[1] One reason is related to the types of inputs and outputs in higher education. Hopkins (1990) points out that for institutions of higher education there are both tangible and intangible inputs and outputs. *Tangible inputs* include such things as the number of new students, faculty time and effort, library holdings, and equipment. *Intangible inputs* include the quality of new students, the quality of the faculty, and so on. *Tangible outputs* include student enrollment in courses, the number of degrees awarded, and the number of scholarly works produced by the faculty. *Intangible outputs* include the quality of instruction provided in courses, the knowledge gained by students over their college career, and the quality of faculty scholarship. Because of these intangible aspects of academic productivity, Hopkins (1990) notes that "all efforts to date at specifying and estimating the higher education production function have provided only partial results" (p. 13). Thus, while we may be able to identify certain inputs and outputs in higher education (i.e., the tangible aspects), capturing productivity in its entirety as some joint result of the tangible and intangible is unlikely at this point. While it can be said that firms in the private sector also must deal with the qualitative aspects of production, I would argue that it is much less of a measurement issue for the private firm given its primary focus on such quantifiable aspects as unit cost and profit maximization.

The problem of being able to only measure tangible activities is further complicated by the fact that the primary activities of most institutions of higher education (instruction, research, and service) are often jointly produced by faculty. Thus, evaluating one specific aspect of production (e.g., contact hours in undergraduate courses) without controlling for the other activities engaged in by the faculty provides an incomplete picture of faculty productivity. Further, increasing the production of one of these activities may come at the expense of the other—referred to as the substitutability effect (Hopkins, 1990). For example, increasing the production of undergraduate instruction results in less research/graduate instruction, and vice versa. In short, assuming no increase in faculty resources, increased faculty productivity in undergraduate education may result in decreased productivity in graduate education and research activities. In fact, one study found that there was a trade-off between teaching productivity and research productivity (Gilmore and To, 1992).[2]

Faculty Productivity Measures

Concerns about the hazards and shortfalls of defining and measuring productivity notwithstanding, there have been three broad categories of measures and indices developed to describe faculty work and its products: faculty activity studies; instructional workload analyses; and measures of noninstructional productivity.

FACULTY ACTIVITY STUDIES. These studies attempt to document the number of hours and/or the proportion of total faculty time spent in major activities such as instruction, research, and service. Analyses of faculty work activities are not new. Yuker (1984) notes that the first study of faculty workloads occurred in 1919. Subsequent studies of this issue have shown a fairly consistent pattern of total hours worked and in the distribution of faculty activity within the traditional tripartite workload model (instruction, research, and service). While there are variations among different types of institutions, disciplines, and instructional staff types, faculty generally report working 50 to 60 hours per week, with approximately one-half of the time devoted to teaching and other instructional activities (Yuker, 1984).

The 1993 *National Survey of Postsecondary Faculty (NSOPF-93)* results were consistent with those of past studies. Full-time faculty at all institutions (public and private) reported spending an average of 59 percent of their time in teaching activities, 16 percent in research, 12 percent in administration, and the remainder in community service and other activities in fall 1992. This distribution varied predictably among the various types of institutions, with faculty at research universities spending more time than average in research and faculty at comprehensive and two-year institutions spending more time than average in teaching activities (see Table 1.1).

Table 1.1 Percentage of Time Full-Time Faculty Spent on Various Activities by Type of Institution, Fall 1992

	Research	Doctoral	Compre-hensive	Liberal Arts	2-Year
Teaching	45.2	53.2	61.1	64.8	70.1
Research and Scholarship	31.0	23.3	13.6	9.6	4.7
Administration	12.2	11.9	12.1	13.8	11.1
Professional Growth	3.3	3.6	4.8	4.5	5.6
Outside Consulting	2.9	2.6	2.8	2.4	2.8
Service and Other	5.3	5.2	5.6	4.7	5.7

From National Center for Education Statistics, *National Survey of Postsecondary Faculty 1993.*

A downside (perhaps unavoidable) to faculty activity studies is in their reliance on self-reported data. While some researchers have argued that the consistency in the findings of faculty activity studies over time lend validity to such data (Jordan, 1994), critics of such data note that it may result in inflated estimates of how much time faculty actually do spend at work or in the distribution of time among their various activities, and thus tend to give low weight to the validity of self-reported data (Miller, 1994; Jordan, 1994).

INSTRUCTIONAL WORKLOAD STUDIES. Another type of faculty productivity analysis focuses on the instructional workload of faculty. Typically such studies focus on such measures as average course loads, contact hours, and credit loads. Again, these studies typically reveal great variance by type of institution, academic discipline, and instructional staff type.

The *NSOPF-93* results also illustrated this variance for two measures of instructional productivity: classroom contact hours and student contact hours (see Table 1.2 below). Classroom contact hours are the number of hours spent teaching group instruction courses, while student contact hours are the number of hours spent teaching group instruction courses multiplied by the total number of students enrolled in those courses. The variance among institutional types is consistent with the pattern of faculty activity illustrated in Table 1.1 where faculty at research and doctoral institutions have lower teaching workloads than faculty at institutions that are predominantly or solely under-graduate in nature.

Table 1.2 Mean Classroom Hours per Week and Mean Student Contact Hours per Week, by Type of Institution, Fall 1992

	Research	Doctoral	Compre-hensive	Liberal Arts	2-Year
Mean Classroom Hours per Week	6.6	8.5	10.7	10.9	16.1
Mean Student Contact Hours per Week	249.6	295.7	316.2	239.0	444.1

Source: From National Center for Education Statistics, *National Survey of Postsecondary Faculty 1993.*

A weakness of such measures of instructional workload is the fact that such measures as average classroom contact hours do not account for the time spent by faculty in preparing for that class, the time spent with students outside of the classroom, or other instruction-related activities. No algorithm is available to provide a reliable estimate of how faculty allocate these elements of their time, nor to estimate the outcomes associated with them.

PRODUCTIVITY IN NONINSTRUCTIONAL ACTIVITIES. Much of what is known about faculty productivity in noninstructional activities is descriptive and is confined to research activities. These analyses tend to focus on such issues as scholarly output as measured by the number of books or articles produced, citations, and the number/dollar value of external grants won.

In summary, the ways of documenting and measuring faculty work have remained relatively unchanged over time. They clearly reflect traditional views of faculty and what faculty do. As documented earlier in this chapter, though, higher education's environment is changing and is likely to be quite different at the turn of the century from even 25 years ago. This raises questions about the specific issues of how to best document and measure what faculty do, as well as the much broader issues of the what, how, and when of faculty work.

THE DISJUNCTURE OF CURRENT CONCEPTIONS OF FACULTY WORK AND PRODUCTIVITY WITH HIGHER EDUCATION'S NEW ENVIRONMENT

This section juxtaposes the current way in which faculty productivity is conceived and measured with higher education's new environment. In particular, it amplifies the previously discussed weaknesses of current faculty work and productivity indices, the disjuncture between faculty culture and the workplace, and disincentives to faculty service, collaboration, and entrepreneurship. Each of these are discussed more fully below.

Weaknesses of Faculty Work and Productivity Indices

As described earlier, the traditional ways of analyzing faculty workload and productivity have a number of limitations. However, there are two in particular that fly in the face of higher education's changing environment. First, the ways in which faculty work is currently measured focus too much on inputs and too little on outcomes. For example, concentrating on measures such as weekly contact hours or average student credit hours says nothing about the quality of instruction provided, or what students ultimately learned. This has added significance given the increased focus of external stakeholders on results. Parenthetically, it is often the external stakeholders (e.g., legislators) who focus most intently on these input measures while simultaneously emphasizing the importance of outcomes. Ironically, then, they may be perpetuating the overuse of such measures by colleges and universities, and ultimately the importance of the input being measured (e.g., time in class and section size).

Second, as noted previously, there is the problem of capturing the intangible inputs and outputs. Measuring the hours spent in a classroom or the number of journal articles produced tells us little about the quality of instruction provided or the quality of the scholarship. Unfortunately, while many have attempted to develop theoretical frameworks incorporating these intangible aspects of academic productivity (e.g., Hopkins, 1990), there have been no empirical studies to test their explanatory usefulness (Gilmore and To, 1992). It is interesting to note here the observations of an individual commenting on faculty workload in 1959: "To the best knowledge of the author, no objective study has ever been made of the relationship between quality of faculty performance and faculty workload. It is not at all certain that such a study could be made" (Hicks, 1960, p.4). A generation later, we are no further along on this particular issue.

Ignoring the Marketplace

As discussed earlier in this chapter, higher education institutions appear to be ignoring the advent of new competitors in the marketplace. However, there is perhaps a more fundamental, and related, problem in the differences between the faculty work culture and the work culture of other organizations. Wallhaus (1996) has constructed a framework specifically contrasting these two cultures as illustrated in Figure 1.7. Clearly, many of the attributes noted under Higher Education Values and Practices in the figure are what add to the intangible positive atmosphere of colleges and universities for many individuals. Such things as autonomy, collegial decision-making processes, and a sense of security and changelessness are highly valued by some in higher education. However, Wallhaus notes that many business leaders feel that other skills need to be taught to students in order to prepare them for the workplace: multidisciplinary problem solving, flexibility, and a tolerance for ambiguity, to name but a few. To accomplish this would take a tremendous fundamental, cultural change for colleges and universities in general, and for faculty in particular. However, *not* to begin to move toward adopting these practices will simply add to the competitive advantage held by nontraditional higher education providers in this marketplace as described earlier.

Figure 1.7 Workplace skill expectations of employers in contrast with higher education values and practices
(From Wallhaus, 1996, p. 7.)

Expectations of Employers	*Higher Education Values and Practices*
Boundarylessness	Modular learning; formal course boundaries
Integration of skills across organization	Independence of the disciplines
Cooperation and teamwork	Competition and individualism
Leadership	Decision making by consensus
Decisiveness	Emphasis on collegiality
Just-in-time training	Formal and extended academic calendars
Flying in formation	Flying solo
Encouraging listening and inventiveness	Protecting the mores of the discipline
Development of interpersonal	Eccentric behavior accepted if not skills encouraged
Tolerance for ambiguity	Precision and stability valued
Ability to change	Clinging to current practices and beliefs

Disincentives to Faculty Service and Collaboration

Two final areas are the current disincentives to faculty service and to collaboration. While these areas are both viewed positively from outside the academy and given significant lip service from within the academy, they are not easily achieved. Part of the reason for this, at least at public colleges and universities, is that administrative barriers are brought about by state statutes and regulations or even institutional policies and procedures. However, a major disincentive is also the lack of tangible rewards for such activities. Clearly, this stems in part from the culture described in the previous section.

A NEW ORGANIZING PRINCIPLE
FOR FACULTY PRODUCTIVITY AND REWARDS

Where do we go from here? Clearly, there is a need for a new organizing principle for addressing the issue of faculty productivity and rewards. The principle that I would propose has two components. The first component involves a renewed partnership between faculty and the public. The second, and related, component organizes the evaluation of faculty productivity and rewards around the common goals held by all institutions of higher education regardless of size or mission: teaching and student learning.

Partnership with the Public

Once we have sifted through the rhetoric, anecdotes, legislative inquiries, the debate about the role of faculty generally comes down to one basic question: What *should* faculty do in their work lives? The public view of higher education is shaped by various desired outcomes including:

- College graduates who can get jobs and advance in their careers
- An education comparable to the tuition charged, and
- Solutions to contemporary social and economic concerns (Layzell, Lovell and Gill, 1996)

In short, public expectations of what faculty *should* do reflect these outcomes, and faculty activities to the contrary add to the scathing diatribes against them.

In Wisconsin, there is a long-standing tradition referred to as the Wisconsin Idea. The corresponding motto of this tradition is that "the boundaries of the University of Wisconsin are the boundaries of the state." The basic premise of this concept is derived from the land grant movement whereby one of the roles of the state university is to extend the fruits of its labor to benefit the social, economic, and cultural life of the state. There are many examples of how the Wisconsin Idea has resulted in improvements in agriculture, health care, education, and state government over the past 100 years that have ultimately benefited the residents of the state. The result of this is that the University of

Wisconsin System is viewed (sometimes parochially) by the citizens of the state as something of a public utility. It would be disingenuous for me to suggest that the political relationship between the university and the state was always simpatico, or that the financial support of the UW System in recent years has been any better than the national patterns described at the beginning of this chapter. However, the fact that the Wisconsin Idea has sustained itself over time as part of the culture of the state is evidence for the broader inherent symbiotic relationship higher education has with the public that supports it financially and otherwise.

It is imperative that faculty begin to renew this relationship with the public if for no other reason than to maintain higher education as a priority for public support. Key to this will be linking faculty activities to the broader objectives of the public as described earlier. Clearly this is a two-way street, and it will only succeed if there is an "infusion of interest and resources from higher education's external constituents" (Layzell, Lovell, and Gill, 1996, p. 102). However, the primary burden of change is on the faculty and their institutions.

New Organizing Framework

Two of the problems in evaluating faculty productivity and rewards are the tendency to look at the issue nonsystemically through the various indices and measures described previously, and also to adopt a one-size-fits-all methodology. What faculty do, how they do it, and the resulting outcomes are part of an interrelated system that is affected by the broader environmental factors affecting colleges and universities. For example, the retention and ultimate success of entering college students is as much related to their academic preparedness at entry as to the quality of their in- and out-of-class educational experiences once enrolled. Further, the modes and emphases of production vary by type of institution. Clearly, the specific expectations for faculty at community colleges are different from those at major research universities.

Figure 1.8 reflects a proposed framework developed during the past year within the University of Wisconsin System for measuring the effectiveness of all UW System institutions in meeting a commonly held goal and objective: teaching and student learning outcomes.[3] The new framework is designed around the core process of teaching and student learning and has applicability to any institution of higher

education. This involves input, process, and outcome variables, and reflects both the best of the values of higher education and the public's goals for higher education. It also recognizes the impact of the inputs to higher education (e.g., funding levels and the quality of incoming students) on its processes and outcomes. A major strength of this model is its ability to recognize and adjust for differences among institutions and institutional types. Institutions ranging from community colleges to major research universities can use this framework to address their specific circumstances.

THE ROLE OF THE FEDERAL GOVERNMENT, STATE GOVERNMENTS, AND INSTITUTIONS IN MOVING TOWARD A NEW ORGANIZING PRINCIPLE

The movement toward this new organizing principle will require the coordinated efforts of the federal and state governments as well as institutions themselves. This section outlines some suggestions for what each can do to meet this need.

The Role of the Federal Government

As described earlier, the primary role of the federal government in shaping higher education has been through the provision of student aid and research funding. Through the 1992 reauthorization of the Higher Education Act, the federal government did attempt to take on a more activist role in higher education issues through its student aid policies via the establishment of state postsecondary review entities (SPREs). The SPRE concept was ultimately doomed to failure in the political process because of concerns from the higher education community over its intrusiveness, it did raise the question of the role of the federal government in issues of institutional quality and effectiveness.

One way in which the federal government could help higher education move toward this principle would be to work with the higher education community to reduce regulatory oversight where possible. Clearly, if higher education institutions are to meet the demands of the next century, they are going to need the flexibility to move quickly and decisively.

Another avenue would be for the federal government to incor-porate a demonstration of institutional commitment to teaching and student learning into research grant criteria. This would not necessarily need to be mandatory, but it would be a symbol for institutions and faculty. It would have the effect of linking researchers more closely to the institution, an improvement on the current situation where these individuals are transients who often see their work as being at best tangential to the daily operations and mission of the institution.

The Role of State Governments

The primary role for states in the future will be to work with institutions of higher education to clarify broad expectations and goals and then provide them with the encouragement, flexibility, and basic level of resources so that institutions can achieve these expectations and goals. While it is unlikely that there will be large infusions of new state resources for higher education, there should be a basic level of financial commitment in order to maintain institutional quality. Although the determination of what comprises a basic level of funding is certainly open to interpretation, it is unfair to expect institutions to achieve the goals set for them when there are inadequate resources.

As with the federal government, state governments can also look for ways in which to relieve the regulatory burden on colleges and universities. In many states, for example, public colleges and universities fall under the same personnel and procurement regulations as other state agencies. These regulations are often viewed as impediments to the flexibility and responsiveness of public institutions by institutional managers, given that they have been designed for state agencies generally and are not reflective of the somewhat unique needs of public colleges and universities. As an example of how one state is addressing the regulatory burden issue, the New Jersey Commission on Higher Education recently completed an audit of various federal, state, and local statutes identified as impeding the "flexibility and productivity" of colleges and universities. The results of this audit and the related recommendations will be used to develop an action plan for regulatory relief for the state's system of higher education.

Additionally, state governments can encourage collaborative activity among faculty at different institutions of higher education by reducing administrative/fiscal barriers that are currently impeding such activities or by providing seed money for collaborative projects. One such example is the Higher Education Cooperation Act (HECA) program that is administered by the Illinois Board of Higher Education. HECA has been in existence since the 1970s and is used to fund collaborative projects between two or more institutions of higher education (public and private). Project proposals are submitted and selected for funding on a competitive basis. Project areas have ranged from those involving collaboration with K-12 schools to economic development initiatives to minority education achievement initiatives. Again, while it is unlikely that states could make significant financial investments in such programs at this point in time, there are possibilities for seed money or matching funds to encourage such activities among faculty and institutions.

The Role of Institutions

Institutions will clearly need to play the most active role in moving toward this new organizing principle. Four potential areas for policy development include post-tenure review; alternative employment options; incentives and rewards geared to institutional priorities; recognition of the faculty life cycle in human resources planning; and the development of new measurements of productivity.

Post-Tenure Review

The road to improved productivity begins with the maximization of faculty talents within the role and mission of the institution. The concept of post-tenure review is designed around the continued maintenance and assessment of faculty resources. Such practices already have been adopted and utilized by various institutions across the country, both public and private. Post-tenure review is the process of reviewing the performance and activities of tenured faculty on a regular basis. The basic premise is that faculty activities and goals should generally correspond with institutional goals and needs, both before and after tenure is granted.

Two key aspects of such practices are the review criteria employed and the linkage of the review to both the institutional mission and the institutional reward structure. In order for such a practice to succeed in a practical sense, the review criteria must be developed as a joint effort between faculty and the institutional administration. Henry Levin (1991) notes that one of the keys to improving productivity in higher education is to develop a clear set of goals for the institution (i.e., faculty and staff) that are clearly linked to the institution's mission and to back them up with incentives. By doing so, faculty are given signals as to the overall priorities of the institution and can act accordingly.

Alternative Employment Options

Institutions will also need to explore alternative employment options for their faculty and staff. One potential option for graduate research institutions would be to develop dual tenure tracks for faculty, one for research/graduate instruction and one for undergraduate teaching. While the tripartite mission of instruction, research, and service has traditionally defined the scope of faculty work, it is not always true that faculty are equally capable in research and teaching. Given limited resources, it might make sense to allow individuals who are more interested/capable in one area than the other to focus their time and energies in that particular area.

A second, related option would be for institutions to develop longer-term, renewable employment contracts for faculty in lieu of tenure. Such employment options might also include monetary and/or nonmonetary incentives for faculty to participate. The criteria for contract renewal would also need to be spelled out very clearly up front for both faculty and institutions. The benefit of this option is that it allows institutions to structure the criteria to link institutional goals and needs with individual performance and interests.

Incentives and Rewards Geared to Institutional Priorities

Institutions will also need to begin developing and enhancing existing incentives for faculty related to institutional priorities. The incentives will differ from institution to institution, of course, given that each institution will have its own unique set of priorities. One area that will be cross-cutting, however, will involve the provision of ongoing support and development in the area of instructional technology usage. Clearly, if faculty are going to make the best use of emerging technologies, they will need to have both the tools and the knowledge of how to use them.

Recognition of the Faculty Life Cycle in Human Resources Planning

Given the potential aging of the faculty described earlier, many institutions may be looking at relatively significant numbers of retirements in the next several years. While some have argued that this will provide additional budgetary flexibility for institutions, it also has the effect of losing some of the most talented and productive faculty, which works against the effectiveness of the institution. Institutions may want to explore alternative retirement options whereby faculty who enter retirement are provided an incentive to come back for a fixed period of time (three to five years). This will allow institutions to maintain continuity in academic departments as well as retain productive faculty who can serve as mentors for younger faculty.

New Ways of Measuring Productivity

Despite the methodological and conceptual problems with current ways of measuring productivity, policymakers and the public will continue to use them absent any better alternatives. Certainly, there will be internal needs for improved measures to evaluate our own efforts, both from the input and output sides of the productivity issue. As previously described, there are a number of weaknesses to current methods of measuring faculty workload and productivity. However, "if members of the higher education community do not develop credible and sophisticated alternatives, the public and its representatives will apply their common sense definitions and categories to the academy, and the fit is often a bad one" (Miller, 1994, p. 12). Measures will have to cover inputs and outputs, both tangible and intangible, and should be objective and methodologically rigorous, but accessible to our external stakeholders. In short, "these analyses must combine hard data with explanatory narrative that is comprehensible to the college educated nonacademic" (p. 13).

So where do we go from here? If we return to our new organizing principle, the measurement must encompass the issues of inputs and outputs, and of maximizing faculty talents within the role and mission of the institution. Johnstone (1993) argues that the focus should be on learning productivity: "Learning productivity relates the input of faculty and staff not to enrollments or to courses taught or to credit or classroom hours assigned, but to learning—i.e., the demonstrated mastery of a defined body of knowledge or skills" (p. 2). This concept shifts the attention from the amount of time faculty spend in the classroom to the learning gained by students in the classroom within a given period of time. Johnstone feels that with the right incentives and structuring of the curriculum, students could learn more in shorter periods of time, resulting in increased productivity. He notes, "Learning is more productive when it masters a given body of skills in less time and/or with less costly inputs" (p. 3). In short, this viewpoint changes the focus on productivity from the input side to the output side. This will require a clear sense of focus and timing in the curriculum as well as clear expectations for faculty.

In short, Johnstone's model views the issue in terms of increased *learning* productivity that is framed by clear expectations and outcomes for both teacher *and* student, and in so doing his model begins to get to the heart of these concerns. In the end, outcomes are the heart of the productivity issue. This is not to say that we should or even can lose track of the traditional inputs to the process. As stewards of public funds, public colleges and universities will have to remain mindful of their resources. However, inputs don't have to be the main focus. Improving the quality and quantity of student learning (with the same inputs) in a faster period of time would be a *real* productivity improvement that could place the focus where it matters most—student outcomes. This does not diminish the role or importance of research or service. It also does not mean that the emphasis on or content of undergraduate education would be the same at every institution. However, it does mean that there needs to be a clear, articulated vision of what undergraduate education is about, the expected role of the faculty therein at every institution, and the development and implementation of measures that reflect this focus.

SUMMARY AND CONCLUSION

It is clear that higher education is entering a new era. To recap, the major trends currently shaping higher education are:

- Stagnating state support and an increased reliance on tuition and fees to finance institutional operating costs
- Increased reliance on student loans in student aid policy
- Increased desire for accountability and linking of funding to institutional performance by external stakeholders
- The advent of instructional technology and distance learning and rising competition from nontraditional providers

The concepts of faculty work, productivity, and rewards that have shaped how institutions of higher education operate the past 50 years are not sufficient to meet the challenges of the new era, and in fact may have significant adverse effects on traditional colleges and universities, financially and otherwise. For example, the increased competition for state funding from all areas of state government is forcing governors and legislatures to view each tax dollar spent from a value-added perspective. If higher education cannot demonstrate that the dollars invested are yielding direct benefits to the state, it may be relegated to fighting for the scraps left over after any new money gets allocated elsewhere. Likewise, if colleges and universities cannot produce the kind of individuals needed by employers in today's competitive business environment, or cannot meet the continuing education needs of their existing employees, businesses will look elsewhere. While the demonstration of these tangible benefits requires effective communication strategies for higher education's external stakeholders, their production ultimately rests on the engine that drives each college and university: faculty and faculty work.

This chapter has proposed a new organizing principle for higher education to meet these challenges that involves the establishment of a new partnership between faculty and the public, as well as a potential framework for evaluating faculty productivity and rewards that is organized around the common goals of teaching and student learning. The first step toward meeting the needs of higher education's external publics involves outreach to those stakeholders to understand their needs, followed by the development of an evaluative framework for demonstrating progress toward meeting these needs. Again, it is the faculty who must ultimately initiate this outreach and who must also help to develop this framework. The federal government, state governments, and institutions all have a potential role in helping higher education move toward this new principle as well. In the end, however, it is the faculty who are ultimately the linchpin to success, and an ongoing dialogue with faculty at all three levels for the development of concrete action plans is needed in order to bring about constructive change.

NOTES

1. The term productivity in this chapter refers to academic productivity only (i.e., what faculty produce).

2. Some economists have hypothesized that if the production of one service supports another, then the joint production of each may be more efficient than producing each one separately—"economies of scope" (Halstead, 1991). Brinkman (1990) notes that there have been few studies of this issue,

although there is some evidence that economies of scope do exist for instruction and research.

3. Although not indicated in the figure, it is recognized that this is a dynamic model where the inputs, processes, and outcomes sometimes overlap, and where there are various feedback loops.

REFERENCES

Brinkman, Paul. (1990). Higher education cost functions. In S. Hoenack and E. Collins (Eds.), *The economics of American universities,* (pp. 107–128.) Albany, NY: State University of New York Press.

California Higher Education Policy Center. (1994, October.) *"Three strikes" law could undermine college opportunity.* San Jose, CA: Author.

College Board. (1995, September.) *Trends in student aid: 1985 to 1995.* Washington, DC: Author.

Finn, Chester E. (1997). The conflicting values of consumers and producers. *Educational Record, 78*(1), 10–16.

Folger, John. (1989, November.) *Designing state incentive programs that work.* Paper presented at National Center for Postsecondary Education Governance and Finance Conference on State Fiscal Incentives, Denver, CO.

Gilmore, Jeffrey, and To, Duc. (1992). Evaluating academic productivity and quality. In C. Hollins (Ed.), *Containing costs and improving productivity in higher education.* (New Directions for Institutional Research Report No. 75, pp. 35–47.) San Francisco: Jossey-Bass.

Halstead, Kent. (1991). *Higher education revenues and expenditures: A study of institutional costs.* Washington, DC: Research Associates of Washington.

Hauptman, Arthur. (1997). Financing American higher education in the 1990s. In D. Layzell (Ed.), *Enrollment management and revenue forecasting: Issues, trends, and methods.* (New Directions for Institutional Research, Vol. 93, pp. 19–36.) San Francisco: Jossey-Bass.

Hicks, John W. (1960). Faculty workload—an overview. In K. Bunnell (Ed.), *Faculty workload: A conference report* (pp. 3–11). Washington, DC: American Council on Education.

Hopkins, David. (1990). The higher education production function: Theoretical foundations and empirical findings. In S. Hoenack and E. Collins (Eds.), *The economics of American universities,* (pp. 11–32). Albany, NY: State University of New York Press.

Johnstone, D. Bruce. (1993, April). *Learning Productivity: A New Imperative for American Higher Education* (SUNY Studies in Public Higher Education, No. 3). Albany, NY: State University of New York.

Jordan, Stephen M. (1994). What we have learned about faculty workload: The best evidence. In J.F. Wergin (Ed.), *Analyzing faculty workload.* (New Directions for Institutional Research Report No. 83, pp. 15–24). San Francisco: Jossey-Bass.

Layzell, Daniel T. and Caruthers, J. Kent. (1995, November.) *Performance funding for higher education at the state level.* Paper presented at the annual meeting of the Association for the Study of Higher Education, Orlando, FL.

Layzell, Daniel T., Lovell, Cheryl, and Gill, Judith I., (1996). Developing faculty as an asset in a period of change and uncertainty. In Codwig, M. (Ed.) *Integrating research on faculty: seeking new ways to communicate about the academic life of faculty* (National Center for Education Statistics, NCES 96–849, pp. 93–110). Washington, D.C.: US Government Printing Office.

Levin, Henry. (1991). Raising productivity in higher education. *Journal of Higher Education,* 62(3), pp. 241–262.

Miller, Margaret A. (1994) Pressures to measure faculty work. In J.F. Wergin (Ed.), *Analyzing faculty workload.* (New Directions for Institutional Research Report No. 83, pp. 5–14). San Francisco: Jossey-Bass.

Mingle, James. (1996, September.) Higher education's shift from a producer-dominated to a consumer-dominated industry. Paper presented at the University of Wisconsin System Institutional Research Conference, Madison, WI.

Mingle, James and Lenth, Charles. (1989). *A new approach to accountability and productivity in higher education.* Denver, CO: State Higher Education Executive Officers.

National Center for Education Statistics (NCES). (1993). *National Survey of Postsecondary Faculty 1993.* Washington, DC: U.S. Government Printing Office.

————. (1996). *Digest of education statistics, 1996* (NCES 96–133). Washington, DC: U.S. Government Printing Office.

National Conference of State Legislatures. (Various years). *State budget actions (various years).* Denver, CO: Author.

National Science Foundation. (1995, February 16). Federal share of academic R&D climbed to 60 percent in FY 1993 *NSF Data Briefs.*

Pew Higher Education Research Program. (1996, November). Rumbling, *Policy Perspectives, 7*(1).

Russell, Alene B. (1992). *Faculty workload: State and system perspectives.* Denver, CO: State Higher Education Executive Officers.

University of Wisconsin System (UW System). (1996a). *1994–95 faculty age distributions in the UW System* (Occasional Research Brief Vol. 96, No. 2.). Madison, WI: UW System Office of Policy Analysis and Research.

———. (1996b, October 10). *A new approach to measuring effectiveness and demonstrating accountability for the UW System.* Discussion paper presented at the meeting of the UW System Board of Regents (agenda item I.3.d), Madison, WI.

Wallhaus, Robert. (1996, March). *The roles of postsecondary education in workforce development: Challenges for state policy.* Paper presented at the February conference of the Wingspread Symposium. Racine, WI.

Yuker, Harold. (1984). *Faculty workload: Research, theory, and interpretation.* ASHE-ERIC Higher Education Research Report No. 10. Washington, DC: Association for the Study of Higher Education.

Zuniga, Robin. (1997). Demographic trends and projections affecting higher education. In D. Layzell (Ed.), *Enrollment management and revenue forecasting: Issues, trends, and methods.* (New Directions for Institutional Research, Vol. 93., pp. 3–18.) San Francisco: Jossey-Bass.

Faculty Productivity and Academic Culture*

William G. Tierney
University of Southern California

Arguably, at no other time throughout this century has faculty work come under the degree of scrutiny that it currently does. If one believes much of the popular literature about the professorate, one logical conclusion would be that the problems that exist in academe rest on the shoulders of the faculty. Faculty have been criticized for being unresponsive to the concerns of society, for focusing on their own research interests rather than the needs of the students, and for sheltering colleagues who do not meet minimal performance standards, to name but three frequent attacks (Kimball, 1990; Sykes, 1988; Chait, 1997).

If faculty are the individuals who many believe need to change, then the faculty reward structure in general, and tenure in particular, is what the critics say is in need of drastic overhaul, if not elimination. If we want faculty to undertake new roles, argue some, we must get rid of the structure that has shielded faculty from the necessity to change—tenure. Change or eliminate tenure, goes the thinking, and the faculty will alter their behavior.

I will suggest here that in part the critics have a point. Organizations are not static entities, but dynamic ones; this is especially the case in a rapidly changing world such as currently exists for

---

*Portions of this text have appeared in William G. Tierney's *Building the Responsive Campus, Creating High Performance Colleges & Universities*.

colleges and universities. Academe is being asked to assume tasks that it has never before considered (Tierney, 1998). If we are to adjust to changing environments, it is well worth our while to consider how we reward individuals and what we think are productive working arrangements.

Accordingly, we might need to reform the roles, responsibilities, and rewards of faculty if we are to meet the changing social, economic, and cultural contexts in which academe works. In arguing such a point, I continue a line of thinking first articulated by Ernest Boyer (1990) and expanded on by Eugene Rice (1996). Both individuals have called for expanded definitions of what we think of as scholarship. Their work forms the scaffolding for this chapter. What I seek here is an extension of their notions about a fuller, more comprehensive definition of faculty work. In essence, my concerns are twofold:

1. If we accept that the academy ought to expand its concept of scholarship, how might we then think of productivity and still maintain a commitment to academic community?
2. If we develop a working definition of productivity that is able to function within the culture of academe, how might we reform the models upon which we currently operate?

Caveat emptor! By reform I do not mean the abolition of tenure. Indeed, the word *reform* means "convert into another and a better form; improvement; radical change for the better" (Onions, 1966, p. 750). It is with such a meaning that I discuss faculty productivity.

This is an essay in the root sense of the word: a trial of some ideas. My aim is to have us rethink what we mean by faculty work and productivity, and in doing so, lessen the vitriolic attacks and improve the climate for change. Over the last five years I have been involved in three research projects that have looked at issues surrounding faculty work, promotion, and tenure. I have interviewed about 300 individuals. I have come away from these interviews with a concern for the tenor and climate of the arguments surrounding academic life. In what follows, I argue a single point: the academy can benefit from a rich array of tasks, roles, and reward strategies for the professorate that will enable them to achieve to their highest potential in a culture based on support, trust, and community.

The text divides in three. I first discuss previous definitions of productivity and raise my own concerns with them. I then suggest alternative ways that a college or university might think about faculty productivity if we work from a cultural perspective. I conclude by discussing what a model of productivity might look like within an organization's culture.

DEFINING PRODUCTIVITY

Perhaps more than in any other occupation, academic life is framed by an overwhelming attention to the language we use in constructing our arguments. The professorate, whether in biology, engineering, or law, is trained in the art of critique. We read articles, participate in oral examinations, and critique colleagues' presentations with an eye toward finding the flaws in one another's arguments. Such a concern spills over into our daily lives with one another and into the governance of the institution. Loose language, imprecise words in a document, or lack of specificity in a text are surefire ways to stymie, if not destroy, a change effort.

A concern for language and how we communicate with one another circumscribes how we approach discussions about faculty productivity. Indeed, the word itself—productivity—is jarring to many, at odds with how professors define their work. My point here is that change agents in the academy do not simply need to educate the faculty—as if when they receive additional information they will see it "my" way; instead, those who promulgate change also need to appreciate and understand the cultural perspective and interpretation of groups different from their own. Thus, in order to concentrate on language about faculty life I provide four common definitions of productivity.

1. "Productivity refers to the way in which a firm transforms inputs (e.g. labor and capital) into outputs" (Layzell, 1996, p. 269).
2. "Learning productivity relates the input of faculty and staff not to enrollments or to courses taught or to credit or classroom hours assigned, but to learning—i.e. the demonstrated mastery of a defined body of knowledge of skills" (Johnstone, 1993, p. 2).
3. "[Productivity] will refer to an increase in educational outcomes (for example, more students served, improved instructional outcomes, a more valued mix of services) relative to costs, or lower costs for a given set of educational outcomes" (Levin, 1991, p. 242).

4. "The economist sees productivity as the ratio of outputs to inputs, [and] faculty focus mainly on the fraction's numerator" (Massy and Wilger, 1995, p. 20).

Now I offer representative quotes from interviews I have done with faculty about how they define productivity when queried.

1. "I look at if someone produces sound work, has high standards for his students, is a good citizen around here."
2. "If you ask me if Professor Jones is productive, I'm likely to say yes if he publishes a lot."
3. "A productive professor is someone who is a good teacher, helps his students learn, inspires them."
4. "Productivity has to do with the contribution you make to the field, to the profession, by what you do—teach, work in the lab."
5. "Am I productive? I guess I'd say yes because I write a lot, but I don't know really, because I work all the time. Doesn't productivity have something to do with efficiency, time on task, that sort of thing? I don't think you can think of academic life that way. It's a calling."
6. "*Productivity* is a stupid word to use when you talk about teaching. Machine workers are productive, or an economy can be productive. What I do in the classroom has less to do with productivity and more to do with quality."

What might we make of these differing definitions of productivity? A first response might be to throw up our hands and see if we can impose tighter measures on faculty to ensure that they adhere to our definition of productivity. This is a view of the world that works from the assumption that one definition exists for a term, and how "we" have defined it is correct. The task of the change agent becomes either convincing or forcing the recalcitrants to adhere to the "correct" definition. The problem with such a strategy in academe is that faculty are remarkably resilient at avoiding administrative attempts to govern their life in such a way.

A second response pertains to the desire to educate. If we explain how faculty work might be thought of as inputs and outputs, the thinking goes, faculty will be better able to understand productivity. Such a comment, however, assumes that faculty see their lives and academic life in the same way that those who propose productivity measures do, and that the use of such language will improve the institution. In effect, we have the same mind-set as in the first response, but the attempt is more benign than hard-edged.

The third response tries to understand the perspective of multiple constituencies and proceeds from there. Surely the use of a word or phrase is not our end goal; rather, our goals ought to be about achieving the mission statement of the institution. If convincing faculty of an idea, rather than a word, becomes important, different questions arise. Why has productivity become an issue? Why are we concerned about defining faculty productivity? What is the problem that we are trying to solve? To answer these questions I first review the workloads of faculty, discuss the professorate's concerns with the idea of productivity, and then consider how productivity fits within an academic culture.

PRODUCTIVITY AND CULTURE

Employment Profiles

Obviously, defining the productivity of a faculty member is a combination of multiple criteria that are both extrinsic to, and defined by, the individual. Minimal standards of teaching excellence, for example, might be developed irrespective of who is teaching. At the same time, we have different expectations of a full professor than of his or her junior counterpart. An individual might face a personal catastrophe during the course of a year that will impact on one's work, but we would be able to contextualize our understanding and decide that given the circumstances, Professor X had a productive year.

A productive faculty member's work will be dramatically different if he or she teaches at a private research university, a comprehensive state university, or a community college. What we expect from a professor of engineering will not be similar to our expectations of a classics professor. We will have different criteria for a part-time professor than for a full-time faculty member. What we expect of someone on the tenure track may well differ from what we desire of a clinical professor who is off the tenure track.

Although we may think such comments are commonsensical, unfortunately throughout this century we have had a desire for an approach that seeks to fit everyone into one mold when it comes to defining productivity. If we exclude community colleges, for example, all institutional types reward research over teaching (Fairweather, 1993; Tierney and Bensimon, 1996). Certainly a professor at a research university might publish more than his or her counterpart at a comprehensive; however, if we compare two individuals at the same institution we will discover that the individual who publishes more will receive a greater reward, as defined by salary increase and/or promotion.

We also argue a great deal over what we expect of tenure-track faculty when the fastest- growing group in the professorate are those who are off the tenure track (Gappa, 1996). Little attention is given to part-time and/or adjunct faculty. We laud on the one hand the amount of time we spend hiring and evaluating a tenure-track professor, and on the other hand we often have a cavalier attitude toward how we hire and evaluate a part-time or non-tenure-track faculty member. One wonders why we would spend so much time defining the productivity of an individual who works in one office and virtually disregard the tenured professor's colleague who happens to work full-time, but is not tenure-track. Indeed, given the rise in non-tenure-track positions, a case might be made that more effort should be spent in evaluating their productivity in so far as most of our traditional criteria (hiring, promotion, and tenure guidelines) are absent.

Judith Gappa (1996, p.2) has pointed out the following:

- Two-thirds of all faculty are full-time.
- Three-fourths of all full-time faculty are tenure-track.
- One-half of all faculty in all institutions are not on the tenure track.
- Full-time faculty hires over the last five years reveal an increasing trend toward hiring non-tenure-track faculty.

The implications here are straightforward. Rightly or wrongly, institutions continue to move toward hiring non-tenure-track faculty in part-time and full-time positions. Evaluative criteria that have been developed over this century have seen a drift toward a "research model" where one's productivity gets measured in terms of research output rather than other criteria such as teaching, service, or direct work in the community. Standardized criteria for hiring and initial evaluation exist for tenure-track professors, but are generally absent for others. There is certainly no grand plan about how to proceed, so what we experience are individualized institutional efforts at resolving problems that I outlined above.

Productivity as Sanction

At the same time that employment profiles are in flux we have had this movement to make faculty more productive in what they do, or rather, what different constituencies (e.g., state legislatures) think faculty should do. However, productivity, as defined above, has a harsh, shrill ring to it that presumably reduces faculty work to a series of managed activities that can be, and must be, monitored and evaluated. The interpretation one frequently takes away from discussions about productivity is that faculty are trying to get away with something, that the professorate has a good life and they do not want anyone to disturb it. We need productivity measures to sanction individuals and to rid ourselves of unproductive personnel.

Productivity, framed in this manner, has two fatal flaws. First, we cannot create long—term, dynamic change in an environment where we scare or demean the general population. Fundamental change in an organization that relies on the active participation of intellectuals occurs where trust is widespread (Tierney, 1998b).

Second, the perception that faculty are lazy or sluggards is simply incorrect. In the research projects I have been involved in (Tierney and Bensimon, 1996; Tierney, 1998a), I discovered faculty who put in remarkably long hours at relatively low pay. The faculty I interviewed frequently work weekday evenings and at least one day on the weekend.

Individuals may not be undertaking tasks that we want them to perform, but that is a different matter. That is, perhaps some institutions should reorient what faculty do so that teaching or engaged work with the external community receives greater emphasis. To do so, however, suggests that we must change the reward structure, not blame individuals as being unproductive. We ought not to lay accusations at people's feet if they are undertaking tasks for which they are rewarded, but we want them to do something else. Instead, we ought to change the reward structure.

Further, at no institution where I have interviewed faculty or administrators have I heard anyone say that deadwood is a significant problem. Sure, each department or school has a war story about an individual who we all judge as unproductive, but the problem is not pervasive. Rather, it can be handled on a case-by-case basis. I know of no company that does not have a problem with a small percentage of its workforce. Disaffected and unproductive employees are a source of concern, but we ought not to tar all individuals with a broad brush stroke that paints everyone as unproductive, or at the least suspect.

PRODUCTIVITY AND CULTURE

In what follows, I first define productivity within an organization's culture. The discussion frames productivity in a fundamentally different way from the previous discussions and concerns we have discussed. I then turn to a model of how we might think about faculty productivity. The model moves away from a unitary one-size-fits-all structure and toward a more multidimensional approach. In this light, some of what follows relates to the older work of Bess (1982) and the more recent scholarship of Paulsen and Feldman (1995). I conclude by considering how we might implement such a model by using what I will call *performance contracts*.

Defining Productivity

John Collier, an anthropologist who spent his life working with Native Americans and studying their struggles over schooling, once wrote:

> I move forward in this writing, as I did in the field experience itself,
> seeking an educational definition that offers people, no matter how
> different from others, a productive place in the modern world. I write
> with conviction that not only are people and peoples inherently
> unique but that civilization is enriched and tempered by this
> diversified vitality. (1973, p. 6)

I resonate with the tone and substance of what Collier wrote. He works from a language of respect, strength, and conviction about individuals, groups, and productivity. How might we apply Collier's words to our discussion?

He begins by saying, "I move forward in this writing, as I did in the field experience itself" Simple enough. Those of us involved in academic change and appraisal may assume the same mantle: "We move forward in the creation of productivity guidelines, as we do in our daily work with one another." The implicit—and critical—point here is that those involved in academic life create the changes, rather than have them imposed from external agents (e.g., state legislatures, boards of trustees, etc.).

He sought "an educational definition that offers people, no matter how different from others, a productive place in the modern world." Various words here are encouraging, reassuring. Collier seeks an "educational" definition. The implication is that multiple definitions exist, but when we speak of educational organizations and processes, we are involved in something special. He also seeks a definition that "offers" people. Consider how dramatically different a definition is that "offers" people rather than "demands of" or "commands" people. We have an emphasis on a framework that places the onus on the organizational community rather than on the individual. A definition that demands is one where I picture the speaker waving his or her finger at me; a definition that offers is one of encouragement.

As opposed to a unitary approach, Collier acknowledges that he wants a definition where individuals "no matter how different from others" may find a "productive place." We have an organizational schema, then, where multiple possibilities exist. Economists will grumble that Collier's use of productive is not what they mean. Precisely. He does not speak of inputs and outputs. His language is one that befits an academic community, and creates a schema that we might employ to ensure high performance.

Indeed, Collier compounds the problem for traditional economists: "I write with conviction that not only are people and peoples inherently unique." Again, his language, infused with hope, ought to find sustenance in our own institutions. We also ought to write with conviction rather than cynicism or vindictiveness. And if we want high performance we must be able to come to terms with defining the best in individuals, rather than seek their weak points in order to expose them.

He concludes by speaking about the importance of such diversity and how civilization is "enriched and tempered by this diversified vitality." Those of us in academe might write that organizations are similarly enriched and tempered. Our struggle is how to put into practice such language. I appreciate that the accountant with the proverbial green eyeshade may be made uncomfortable with discussions about productivity that begin with convictions, offer multiple opportunities for people, and suggest that the emphasis ought to be on the community creating the conditions for high performance. An easier, albeit unsuccessful, way to go is to create productivity indices within the confines of my office, publish them, and then watch to see who can and cannot jump over the bars I have set.

Productivity in an academic community begins from dramatically different premises from where the discussion has taken us up to this point. Productivity ought not to be a bureaucratic search for indicators so that we are able to reward some and sanction others. If an academic community exists where we seek to find a productive place for individuals, then we might develop productivity indicators with two key goals in mind. First, productivity ought to be something that is an ongoing activity that we think about throughout an academic year. Simply stated, if we plant a garden, the health and beauty of our fruit are determined not when we pick them, but by the processes we use to grow them, the care we demonstrate at nurturing them.

As a member of the academic community, I also have an obligation to the community. My responsibility to teach to the best of my ability, for example, ought to be measured not because there is an obscure chart that needs to be filled in for state agencies, but because I have communal relationships with my colleagues that necessitate we perform well for one another. Productivity is not a bureaucratic measure for individual excellence, but the vehicle that offers faculty particular rights and responsibilities.

Thus, if academe is a community in search of high performance, then we need to focus more centrally on how productivity is an ongoing developmental activity. The discussions move away from defining the problem as deadwood or how tenure is an impediment to change (Tierney, 1997). Instead, we focus our attention on improving the culture of faculty life by discussing in depth—honestly, concretely, personally—how we as a faculty, and myself as an individual, might improve. Productivity in this manner moves away from a culture of fear and retribution, and toward an understanding of how we might achieve the diversity that Collier defined. The challenge, of course, is how to implement a climate for improvement.

A Model for Change

At present we have models of productivity that ostensibly mirror the way an institution has configured three separate and distinct tasks—teaching, service, and research. (See figure 2.1). We have developed ways to assess whether an individual is an adequate teacher, researcher, and university citizen. We also provide arbitrary judgments about the weight someone should give to each activity. At a research university, for example, a professor usually must emphasize research and downplay service. At a liberal arts college, teaching may be accorded equal status to research. We also increasingly try to tie each discrete activity to the organization's mission and goals.

Figure 2.1 Traditional Framework for Faculty Work

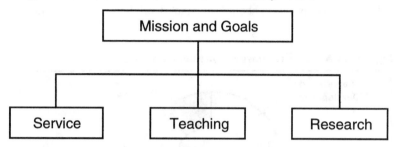

One ought not to be surprised about how our assessment has evolved insofar as it echoes how we have thought about academic work. Work in one area presumably does not support or feed into another area. The ability to cordon off activities in this way also allows for judgments to be made based on standardized benchmarks about what we are all to do. That is, if an institution states that all faculty ought to spend 40 percent of their time on research, then we presumably are able to judge one individual against another to see how one measures against his or her peers. Although the model is not necessarily competitive, it most assuredly is based on the assumption that all faculty should be engaged in similar activities and participate with similar emphases.

The problem, of course, is that I have pointed out how the academic world is changing. We need more diversity, not less; we need more possibilities to tap into individual strengths rather than try to force everyone into one model. At the same time, there are core activities that exist in the organization—teaching, research, and service—but rather than isolate them from one another, what we might do is think about how they fit together.

If we work from the assumptions that I have developed from Collier's definition, three points emerge. First, we need a model that tries to conjoin, rather than isolate, activities. Second, one's work in an organization's culture ought not to be indirectly related to the mission and goals, but central. And third, different faculty will have different work profiles.

In Figure 2.2 I have attempted to portray how we might reconceptualize faculty work. One point of the sketch is that the mission and goals of the organization are at the core, rather than on the periphery. The second point is that instead of being isolated from one another in boxes we think of our work as related. And the third point is that an individual has discretion about how much work he or she might do in any one area.

Figure 2.2 A New Framework for Faculty Work

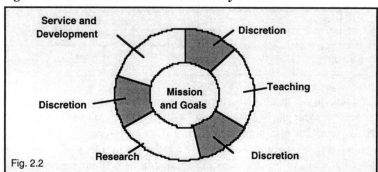

Fig. 2.2

Presumably, the organization would come to agreement about basic criteria, and then each individual will see how he or she will depart from the criteria. The words, also, might be different from institution to institution. Some institutions may well keep the traditional trinity of research, teaching, and service, but I also anticipate that some institutions might prefer to think of service as community outreach and governance. Others might substitute scholarship for research. The challenge is twofold. By working from a model such as I have suggested, we first must define faculty work as it relates to the specific goals and vision of our own college or university, rather than assume that we all must meet the same standard. Once we have agreed on broad organizational goals, we then need to figure out how we might assess each individual's productivity.

Performance Contracts

In an earlier section I raised two issues that are relevant here. First, often we do not evaluate the performance of non-tenure-track faculty. Second, productivity is often tied to merit raises and little more.

Performance contracts should be for all faculty. Performance contracts have been debated off and on for a number of years. The retrenchment issues of the 1970s brought forth suggestions for performance contracts, as did a spate of literature on management by objectives. The difference with what is suggested here is processual. We develop a contract primarily as a way to enable individuals to set goals for themselves and to announce to the community how their work enhances the strategic plan and mission of the organization according to what the institution has devised for its own version of the model shown in Figure 2.2. The model that I have outlined enables great leeway in what an individual intends to do, and what we will reward. As a by-product we will be able to reward those who are high performers and perhaps reconfigure contracts for those few who have not performed well. How might such an activity occur?

First, one's work may invariably change over the course of an academic year. A colleague may abruptly leave and I may be asked to teach a course. Someone may invite me to participate in an edited book for which I had not planned. A performance contract, then, should not be so constrictive that there is not room for capitalizing on unforeseen opportunities.

As I noted above, the faculty develop the model and decide how much effort one might expend in one area or another. There are broad guidelines rather than unitary rules. Once we have such guidelines, we then develop criteria upon which we might base one another's work. A teaching portfolio is one step in the right direction, but there are a multitude of evaluative measures that might be taken that enable faculties to define and evaluate the criteria for performance upon which an individual desires to be judged.

However, once we have standardized criteria that have been developed and approved by the faculty, we have a form to gauge one's performance over the past 12 months. A performance contract delineates what an individual intends to do over the next 12 months. Obviously, some contracts are simple and straightforward. An individual will list the number of courses that he or she has planned, describe the research that is intended, and list the committees on which he or she will participate. In some cases, however, an individual will have a record of conducting no research so one might think that the performance contract might incorporate more teaching to compensate for lack of performance in the other area. If the expectation is that faculty will have a specific advising load and an individual does not meet the load, then the contract would specify how the individual intends to make up the work in another area.

In a community concerned with development and quality, we have an obligation to outline where we intend to go, and how we intend to get there. The point is to ensure that all individuals have productive roles, that everyone is able to work to his or her highest capacity, and that the community supports the actions of one another. If we develop performance contracts, then how we currently think of administration and what we currently conceive of as faculty roles and responsibilities also shifts.

CONCLUSION

We have worried for the greater part of this decade about the future of tenure and how to reform faculty work. Implicitly, I have suggested here that tenure is not the issue. Instead, our challenge lies in developing ways to think of productivity as it relates to academic life, and then implementing a schema that enables individuals to succeed to their highest ability.

I have pointed out the problems with typical definitions of productivity and offered an understanding of productivity from a cultural perspective. I then considered ways to unite academic work rather than isolate one's tasks from others', and suggested how we might make concrete what we expect of one another. To be sure, the model's flexibility is also its greatest worry. Standardized measures that cut across categories, groups, and institutional types are easy to understand, however flawed. But the future of academic life cannot rely on easy assumptions that we all should be doing similar tasks in similar ways. The model developed here surely is not a panacea for the problems that confront us, but hopefully points us in a direction where we are able to tap into our strengths, rather than exploit one another's weaknesses.

REFERENCES

Boyer, Ernest. (1990). *Scholarship reconsidered: Priorities of the professorate.* Princeton, NJ: Carnegie Foundation for the Advancement of Teaching.

Chait, Richard. (1997, July–August). Rethinking tenure. *Harvard Magazine, 99*(6), 30–31, 90.

Collins, James C., and Porras, Jerry I. (1994). *Built to last: Successful habits of visionary companies.* New York: Harper Business.

Fairweather, James S. (1993). Academic values and faculty rewards. *Review of Higher Education, 17*(1), 43–68.

Gappa, Judith M. (1996). Off the tenure track: Six models for full-time, nontenurable appointments. *New Pathways: Faculty Careers and Employment for the 21st Century, 10.*

Johnstone, D. Bruce. (1996, Autumn). Learning productivity: Some key questions. *Learning Productivity News, 1*(2), 1–3.

Kimball, R. (1990). *Tenured radicals: How politics has corrupted our higher education.* New York: Harper and Row.

Layzell, Daniel. (1996). Faculty workload and productivity: Recurrent issues with new imperatives. *Review of Higher Education, 19*(3), 267–282.

Levin, H.M. (1991). Raising productivity in higher education. *Journal of Higher Education, 62*(3), 242–262.

Massy, William, and Wilger, Andrea. (1995, July/August). Improving productivity: What faculty think about it—and its effect on quality. *Change, 27*(4), 10–20.

Onions, C.T. (1966). *The Oxford dictionary of English etymology.* London: Oxford University Press.

Rice, R.E. (1996). *Making a place for the new American scholar.* New Pathways: Faculty Careers and Employment for the 21st Century, Working Paper Series, No. 1. Washington, DC: American Association for Higher Education.

Sykes, C.J. (1988). *ProfScam: Professors and the demise of higher education.* New York: St. Martin's Press.

Tierney, William G. (1997, May–June). Academic community and post-tenure review. *Academe, 83*(3), 23–25.

Tierney, William G. (1998a). *The responsive university: Restructuring for high performance.* Baltimore, MD: Johns Hopkins University Press.

Tierney, William G., (1998b). *Building the responsive campus: Creating high performance colleges and universities.* Thousand Oaks, CA: Sage Publishers

Tierney, William G., and Bensimon, Estela Mara. (1996). *Promotion and tenure: Community and socialization in academe.* Albany, NY: State University of New York Press.

CHAPTER 3

The Highly Productive
Faculty Member
Confronting the Mythologies of Faculty Work

James S. Fairweather
Michigan State University

INTRODUCTION

The historical record strongly suggests that fundamental shifts in demographics and in state and federal policies can change colleges and universities in profound ways. The Morrill Land Grant Act of the 1860s established new types of colleges with distinct missions. The GI Bill of the 1940s resulted in thousands of new students entering colleges and universities. The creation of the National Science Foundation and increased funding following World War II and *Sputnik* made the expansion of academic research possible (Geiger, 1986).

Today academic leaders face another fundamental shift in external policy, one aimed at the internal workings of colleges and universities. Increasing costs and the adverse consequences for access, declining need for large-scale defense-based research, and anxiety about the employment and career consequences of a highly competitive global economy have combined to lead the public—particularly parents and legislators—to ask critical questions about the *nature of faculty work:*

This research was supported by a grant from the Office of Educational Reform and Improvement, U.S. Department of Education (Award No. R309F60075). The views expressed in this paper are solely those of the author.

Academic institutions today face two primary criticisms, each posing
questions about faculty roles and each potentially adversely affecting
institutional autonomy. The first is the belief that faculty in American
colleges and universities, protected by a tenure system, have little
understanding of the vagaries of the marketplace and the anxiety a
rapidly changing economy creates for the populace at large. Fair or
not, this criticism implies that academic institutions and their faculty
should respond more directly to assist the nation and its youth in
responding to changes in the economy. Relatedly, the perception of a
faculty "elite" who follow self-determined research and teaching
agendas has led to criticism about the way in which faculty spend
their time. (Fairweather, 1996, p. 3)

Of growing concern among state legislatures is faculty
productivity, especially with respect to teaching. Recent efforts to
eliminate tenure by the governing boards in Arizona and Florida,
legislation in Ohio to mandate an increase in the time faculty spend on
teaching, and growing legislative interest in post-tenure review are
specific expressions of this concern. The focus of this reform
movement is not limited to public institutions. The National Science
Foundation, which supports and influences both public and private
institutions, recently required grant applicants to state how their
research work will affect their teaching effort.

The willingness and ability of academic institutions to respond
effectively to these challenges is influenced by what Clark (1972) calls
institutional sagas. These sagas contain a variety of beliefs or myths
that help perpetuate organizational culture by socializing new
participants (students, administrators, and especially the faculty) in part
by establishing norms for their behavior. One such norm, the widely
held belief that the key to academic reform lies in the collective
decisions by faculty and administrators (Clark, 1963), potentially can
thwart attempts by legislators, agencies, and public critics to influence
faculty work. Indeed, academic leaders often view legislative efforts
and critical news stories as public relations problems rather than as
indications of an actual need for reform (Bok, 1992). Such a response is
counterproductive when the stimulus for change is a fundamental
societal restructuring (Ashby, 1974).

Academic leaders who promote reform in faculty work face an
even greater barrier to change, namely, a set of beliefs held by many
academic administrators and faculty members about the nature of

faculty work. Among these basic tenets are that (a) teaching, research, and service are activities imbedded in some form within each faculty member's work effort, (b) teaching and research are mutually reinforcing, and as a consequence, (c) faculty can simultaneously be productive in teaching and research.

In this chapter, I examine three widely held tenets of faculty work. The first is the belief that the psychosocial roots of intrinsic motivation is the key to understanding faculty behavior. The second is that teaching and research are mutually reinforcing. The third is the notion that all aspects of faculty work—teaching research, and service—can be equally (or somewhat equally) addressed by the work of each faculty member. Each faculty member is expected to be (and can be) the complete faculty member—productive in both teaching and research. I conclude with a discussion of the policy implications of research findings.

BELIEFS ABOUT FACULTY WORK

Faculty Motivation and Choice

Finkelstein's (1984) review of the literature documents the tradition of viewing faculty behavior as a function of individual social experiences and psychological characteristics. Blackburn and Lawrence (1995) epitomize this perspective in their model of faculty productivity. Their model places the greatest emphasis on self-knowledge, which includes personal interest, commitment, efficacy, psychological characteristics, satisfaction, and morale. Less important according to Blackburn and Lawrence is social knowledge, which includes social support, perceived institutional preference, and institutional values (e.g., rewards). Environmental influences have a tertiary role in their model.

Other authors also have emphasized the psychological and behavioral implications of faculty experiences. Bess (1978), Clark (1987), and Clark and Corcoran (1986) claim that experiences during graduate school help shape the future faculty member's attitudes and behavior. Alpert (1985), Baldwin and Blackburn (1981), Boice (1992), and Reynolds (1992) claim that experiences during the early part of the faculty member's career also affect psychological development and orientation, and thereby influence behavior.

The evidence in support of the intrinsic model of faculty behavior is less convincing than the arguments made in its behalf. Blackburn and Lawrence (1995), the leading proponents of this model, found that the most important factors in faculty research productivity were demographic characteristics (e.g., rank) and "behaviors." The latter category includes obtaining external research funding, which some authors claim is a research productivity measure in its own right (e.g., Konrad and Pfeffer, 1990). In other studies of faculty teaching and research behavior, respectively, Fairweather and Rhoads (1995) and Diamond (1993) found rewards, not socialization or attitudes, to be the strongest correlate of faculty behavior.

Teaching and Research: Mutually Reinforcing

As Crimmel (1984) points out, the teacher-scholar represents the ideal in American higher education. The belief in the teacher-scholar rests on several tenets:

> Teaching and research are seen as mutually reinforcing. From this perspective, the best scholars are the best teachers; the best teacher is a scholar who keeps abreast of the content and methods of a field through continuing involvement in research and who communicates knowledge and enthusiasm for a subject to students. (Fairweather, 1996, p. 100)

Feldman (1987) examined the theoretical bases for believing that research and teaching are mutually reinforcing behaviors. Most are versions of Linsky and Straus's (1975) spillover effect, where, for example, faculty who conduct research are supposedly more likely to introduce research-based material into their classroom instruction. Feldman's (1987) review of more than 200 research studies found little relationship between student ratings of teaching excellence and various forms of research productivity (overall correlation coefficient of .12). Hattie and Marsh (1996) expanded Feldman's analysis and found an even smaller cross-study correlation (.06). As I did before them (Fairweather, 1993), Hattie and Marsh found a negative relationship between faculty time allocated to teaching and time allocated to research.

In contrast, Colbeck's (1997) recent work, using in-depth investigation of a small number of faculty, found that teaching and research activities can overlap but in very specific ways. For example, research is much more likely to overlap with independent study instruction or dissertation committee work than to enhance classroom teaching. By implication, Feldman's and Hattie and Marsh's analyses did not find a relationship between teaching and research because they focused on only one aspect of the instructional work effort (i.e., classroom instruction). In any case, "the common belief that research and teaching are inextricably intertwined is an enduring myth" (Hattie and Marsh, 1996, p. 529).

The Complete Faculty Member

The ultimate tenet about faculty work, which is influenced by beliefs about the importance of intrinsic motivation and the overlap of teaching and research, is that faculty members can be productive in all aspects of faculty work. This belief is codified in promotion and tenure dossiers where faculty members are required to demonstrate their productivity in teaching and research (with some emphasis on service as well).

The belief that the typical faculty member can simultaneously achieve high or at least above average levels of productivity in both research and teaching is largely unexamined. Feldman (1987) and Hattie and Marsh (1996) examined ratings of teaching effectiveness, which is one measure of quality but not of productivity. Much of my work (e.g., Fairweather, 1993, 1996) focuses on time allocation and rewards rather than on specific measures of productivity. Massy and Wilger (1995) discuss faculty perceptions of both teaching and research productivity, but do not demonstrate empirically how this relationship plays out among a national sample of professors.

RESEARCH QUESTIONS

Much of the policy debate about the nature of faculty work is shrouded in its reliance on myths, opinions, and conjectures. The purpose of this chapter is to examine empirically the principal beliefs about faculty work to inform the debate about how to increase faculty productivity, enhance the attention paid to teaching, and preserve the parts of academic life essential to carry out the multiple missions of teaching, research, and service. Specifically, this study examines faculty teaching and research productivity via three questions:

- *Research Question 1:* How productive are the faculty in teaching and research?
- *Research Question 2:* What percentage of the faculty are productive in teaching and research?
- *Research Question 3:* What distinguishes faculty members who are

highly productive in teaching and research from their less
productive colleagues?

THE STUDY

Data for this research were gathered in the 1992–93 *National Survey of
Postsecondary Faculty (NSOPF 1993)*, sponsored by the National
Center for Education Statistics. *NSOPF 1993* examined a nationally
representative sample of 29,764 part-time and full-time faculty in 962
two- and four-year colleges and universities. In all, 25,780 full- and
part-time faculty from 817 institutions responded (respective
institutional and individual response rates of 84.9 percent and 86.6
percent). The institutional sample was stratified by source of control
(public or independent) and by type of institution. Based on the
Carnegie Foundation classification scheme (Carnegie Foundation for
the Advancement of Teaching, 1987), types of institution ranged from
research universities, whose faculty train the majority of doctorates in
the United States and which house most of the funded research;
doctorate-granting universities, whose faculty also train doctoral
students and conduct research but whose production of doctorates and
research dollars generated are less than those of the research universities; *comprehensive colleges and universities,* which focus on liberal
arts and professional programs at the undergraduate and master's
degree levels; *liberal arts colleges,* which focus on teaching undergraduates (although the majority now also offer some type of master's
degree program); *other four-year institutions,* which in this study
primarily focus on separate medical and engineering schools; and *two-
year colleges.* For this research, I used weighted data[1] on *full-time,
tenure-track faculty* from four-year institutions (*n* = 7,835, weighted *n*
= 269, 789). The weighted distribution of faculty by type of four-year
institution is as follows: 35.0 percent from research universities, 15.3
percent from doctorate-granting universities, 34.9 percent from
comprehensive colleges and universities, 8.4 percent from liberal arts
colleges, and 6.4 percent from other four-year institutions.

METHODS

For Research Question 1, weighted means and variances were
calculated for selected measures of research and teaching output. T-
tests were used to compare mean differences on these output measures
by type of institution, program area, gender, race/ethnicity, and

academic rank. Research Question 2 first required defining three teaching/research "productivity" groups based on a single measure of research productivity (refereed publications during the previous two years) and on three different measures of instructional output (total instructional productivity, percentage of time spent on teaching, and use of collaborative instructional approaches in the classroom). The weighted percentages of faculty falling into these high performing groups then were calculated. For faculty who were above average in both publishing and total instructional productivity (Group 1), logistic regression analyses using weighted data were used to identify the factors that distinguish highly productive teacher-researchers from their counterparts (Research Question 3).

THE MODEL

Defining a Highly Productive Faculty Member

The first step in identifying faculty members who are highly productive in teaching and research is to select appropriate productivity or output measures. The measures selected must have meaning across all types of four-year institutions and permit comparison with previous research. The measure of *research productivity* that meets these criteria is the *number of refereed publications during the previous two years,* where "publications" include articles in refereed journals; published reviews of books, articles, or creative works; books; textbooks; monographs; and chapters in edited volumes.[2] Publishing productivity has the advantage of having similar meaning and value across types of institution, at least as reflected in faculty rewards (see Fairweather, 1996). It also has been widely used in previous research, ranging from Ladd (1979) to Blackburn and Lawrence (1995).

Less agreement exists on an appropriate measure of *instructional productivity.* Researchers and policymakers often confuse teaching productivity, quality, effectiveness, and time allocation, and mistake faculty input (e.g., hours spent teaching) for student learning outcomes. Johnstone (1993) appropriately points out that any measure of faculty instructional productivity may not reflect student learning productivity. This limitation should be kept in mind in the following discussion.

Consistent with previous literature, I chose three distinct measures related to instructional output to help define highly productive teachers. The first is a true productivity measure, *total instructional productivity.* This measure is the sum of the number of *student classroom contact hours per week* and the number of *independent study contact hours per week*.[3]

The second measure of instructional output is not a measure of productivity but of time allocation: *percentage of time spent on teaching*. Used by many authors previously (e.g., Baldridge, Curtis, Ecker, and Riley, 1978; Fulton and Trow, 1974; Fairweather and Rhoads, 1995), time spent on teaching includes time spent on teaching, grading papers, and preparing courses; developing new curricula; advising or supervising students; and working with student organizations or intramural athletics. This measure of time allocation includes both work assignment, such as class teaching load, and commitment to teaching, such as additional effort devoted to curriculum reform (Fairweather and Rhoads, 1995). It does not, however, imply a measure of quality.

The third measure of instructional output focuses on classroom teaching methods. The emphasis here is on anticipated student learning outcomes. Recent literature indicates that students exposed to collaborative or active learning experiences may learn more than those whose classroom experience is passive (Bruffee, 1993; Goodsell, Maher, and Tinto, 1992; Weimer, 1990, 1996). Based on this literature, for each class taught during fall term 1992, I deemed a faculty member who used any of the following approaches as his or her primary instructional method as using a collaborative instructional approach in that class: discussion group and class presentations; apprenticeship, internship, field work, or field trips; role-playing, simulation, or other performances; group projects; or cooperative learning groups. Lectures, seminars,[4] or television were defined as noncollaborative forms of primary instructional approaches.[5] The *ratio of use of collaborative learning as the primary instructional approach to the total number of courses taught in fall term 1992* was used to estimate each faculty member's use of collaborative instructional techniques. A faculty member who taught five courses, four using lecture as the primary instructional approach and one using group projects, had a collaborative instruction ratio of 1/5 or .20. Faculty members whose ratio exceeded zero were deemed to have demonstrated some evidence of the use of collaborative learning as a primary instructional approach.

Using these measures of research productivity and instructional output, I defined *highly productive researchers* as being above average on refereed publications during the past two years for their discipline and type of institution. Depending on the measure, I defined *highly productive teachers* as being above average in total instructional productivity for their discipline and type of institution, above average in time spent on teaching for their discipline and type of institution, or showing evidence of using a collaborative approach as the primary classroom instructional technique. I used these definitions to form three groups of high producing teacher-researchers:

• *Group 1:* Above average in research productivity/above average in total instructional productivity
• *Group 2:* Above average in research productivity/above average in time spent on teaching
• *Group 3:* Above average in research productivity/some use of collaborative instruction

Consider education faculty in research universities. These faculty averaged 6.231 refereed publications during the previous two years, 41.374 percent of time spent on teaching (fall term 1992), and 212.27 total contact hours with students per week (fall term 1992). Education faculty from research universities who had seven or more publications during the previous two years and who had more than 212 total student contact hours per week were classified as highly productive according to the definition for Group 1. Education faculty who had seven or more publications during the previous two years and who spent more than 41 percent of their time on instruction were classified as highly productive according to the definition for Group 2. Education faculty who had seven or more publications during the previous two years and who had a collaborative ratio greater than zero (i.e., indicating at least some use of a collaborative technique as the primary instructional approach during fall term 1992) were classified as highly productive according to the definition for Group 3.[6] This process was repeated for faculty members in each discipline and type of institution.

Factors Affecting Faculty Productivity

Using only Group 1 (based on true productivity measures), for Research Question 3 I developed a model of faculty productivity to identify factors that distinguish high performing faculty from their counterparts. I used a modified version of the model used by Fairweather and Rhoads (1995) (see Figure 3.1). The model included the following components:

- *The criterion* was productivity group membership (yes or no for belonging to Group 1).
- *Controls* included institutional-level measures of *size* (full-time equivalent enrollment) and *wealth* (education and general expenditures), *academic discipline,*[7] and *personal demographics* (gender, race/ethnicity, and academic rank).
- *Early socialization* (Bess, 1978; Clark, 1987; Clark and Corcoran, 1986) was measured by whether or not the faculty member had been a *teaching assistant in graduate school; highest degree/prestige; previous college teaching experience* (i.e., previous employment at a four-year college or university where the primary focus of the position was on teaching); and *previous college research experience* (i.e., previous employment at a four-year college or university where the primary focus of the position was on research).
- *Current socialization/self-motivation* (Alpert, 1985; Baldwin and Blackburn, 1981; Blackburn and Lawrence, 1995; Boice, 1992; Reynolds, 1992) includes *the importance of reducing the pressure to publish in the faculty member's decision to change jobs* to estimate a faculty member's attitude toward teaching. I used *agreement with publishing being the primary criterion for promotion and tenure* and *the importance of good research facilities/equipment in the faculty member's decision to change jobs* to estimate attitudes toward research.
- *Work allocation* (Austin, 1992) includes *hours in class per week* and whether or not the faculty member *taught only graduate students.*
- Measures of *departmental climate and resources* (Bland and Schmitz, 1986) include *satisfaction with the authority to choose classes to teach, adequacy of personal computers for personal use,* and *adequacy of library facilities.*
- The model includes indicators of *perceived* and *actual rewards* (Diamond, 1993; Fairweather, 1996). The former is measured by agreement with the statement *"at this institution research is rewarded more than teaching."* The latter is measured by *basic salary during the academic year.*
- Specific components of *productivity* may affect other components of it. For example, *number of externally funded grants during fall term 1992 for which the faculty member was principal or co-principal investigator* and *number of conference presentations*

during 1990–92 could affect publishing productivity. *Number of thesis or dissertation committees served on during fall term 1992* could affect classroom productivity.

Figure 3.1 Faculty productivity model

Controls
   Institution
      FTE enrollment (size)
      Education and general expenditures (wealth)
   Discipline
   Personal
      Gender (0 = female, 1 = male)
      Race/ethnicity (0 = non-minority, 1 = minority)
      Academic Rank (scale: professor to lecturer/instructor)
Early Socialization
   Teaching assistantship in graduate school (0 = no, 1 = yes)
   Highest degree/prestige (0 = no doctorate or equivalent,
         1 = doctorate or equivalent from non-research I university,
         2 = doctorate or equivalent from Research I university)
   Previous college teaching experience (0 = no, 1 = yes)[a]
   Previous college research experience (0 = no, 1 = yes)[b]
Current Socialization/Self-motivation
   Teaching
      If respondent left present institution, importance of no pressure
         to publish (1 = not important, 2 = somewhat important,
         3 = very important)
   Research
      Agree that research/publication should be the primary criterion for
         promotion and tenure at this institution (from 1 = strongly disagree
         to 4 = strongly agree)
      If respondent left present institution, importance of good research
         facilities/equipment (1 = not important, 2 = somewhat important,
         3 = very important)
Work Allocation
   Hours in class/week
   Taught only graduate students (0 = no, 1 = yes)
   Department chair (0 = no, 1 = yes)

(continued next page)

Figure 3.1 Faculty productivity model *(continued)*

Climate/Resources

> Satisfied with authority to choose classes to teach
>> (from 1 = very dissatisfied to 4 = very satisfied)
>
> Adequacy of personal computers for personal use
>> (from 1 = very poor, to 4 = very good)
>
> Adequacy of university library facilities
>> (from 1 = very poor to 4 = very good)

Rewards

> At this institution, research is rewarded more than teaching
>> (from 1 = strongly disagree to 4 = strongly agree)
>
> Basic salary (log)

Productivity Predictors

> *Research*
>> Number of grants on which respondent was principal or co-principal investigator, fall 1992
>>
>> Number of presentations at conferences in the past two years
>
> *Teaching*
>> Student contact hours/week
>>
>> Number of independent study contact hours/week
>>
>> Number of thesis or dissertation committees served on, fall 1992

Productivity-Related Criteria

> *Research*
>> Number of refereed publications during previous two years[c]
>
> *Teaching*
>> Total instructional productivity[d]
>
> *Time Allocation*
>> More time on research, less on teaching[e]
>
> *Instructional Approach*
>> Ratio of collaborative instruction as primary teaching approach to total number of courses taught

---

[a] Primary job was teaching.

[b] Primary job was research.

[c] Refereed articles, published book reviews, books, monographs, chapters in edited books

[d] Student classroom contact hours plus independent study contact hours

[e] Percentage of time spent on research minus percentage of time spent on teaching

RESULTS

Research Question 1: How productive are the faculty in teaching and research?

Publishing productivity ranged from a high of about six refereed publications during the previous two years for faculty members in research universities, to a low of less than two publications during the same time period for faculty in liberal arts colleges (see Table 3.1).[8] Faculty who work in liberal arts colleges produced the least number of total student contact hours in fall term 1992 (signifying smaller class sizes), whereas faculty members in other four-year institutions produced significantly larger numbers of contact hours.[9] Faculty members in research and other four-year institutions spent the least time on teaching—about 40 percent. Their colleagues in doctorate-granting

Table 3.1 Distribution of Group-Defining Variables, by Type of Institution

Type of Institution	Publishing, 2-Year		Total Instructional Productivity		Time Spent, Teaching (%)		Collaborative Instruction Ratio	
	Mean	SE[a]	Mean	SE	Mean	SE	Mean	SE
All 4-Year	3.89	.063	323.31	5.080	51.63	.286	.16	.004
Research	6.02	.175	311.15	13.905	40.19	.588	.13	.009
Doctoral	3.97	.126	324.34	11.705	50.44	.605	.15	.009
Comprehensive	2.05	.064	328.55	5.987	61.55	.381	.19	.006
Liberal Arts	1.69	.110	247.15	7.891	66.98	.771	.21	.013
Other 4-Year	5.01	.299	481.04	32.115	41.93	1.256	.14	.017

Source: Adapted from NSOPF 1993.

[a] SE = standard error

institutions spent about one-half of their time on instruction. Faculty in comprehensive and liberal arts colleges spent the most time on instruction (more than 60 percent).[10] The average ratio of collaborative instructional techniques to the number of courses taught during fall term 1992 was highest in the more teaching-oriented institutions (about .20) and lowest in the more research-oriented institutions (ranging from .13 in research universities to .15 in doctorate-granting universities).[11]

Publishing productivity ranged by program area from 1.38 publications per two-year period in fine arts to 5.49 in health sciences (see Table 3.2). Faculty in business, education, fine arts, the humanities, and other fields produced below average numbers of publications; faculty in engineering, health sciences, and natural sciences were above average.[12]

Total instructional productivity ranged from a high of about 304 student contact hours for faculty in health sciences to a low of about 224 in engineering. Faculty in the health sciences produced a much greater number of contact hours than did their counterparts in other program areas.[13] Faculty in education, fine arts, the humanities, and other fields spent significantly more of their time on teaching than the national norm; faculty in agriculture, engineering, and health sciences spent below average percentages of their time on teaching.[14] The use of collaborative instruction varied substantially by academic discipline. Faculty in fine arts, education, and the humanities were the most likely to use collaborative techniques; faculty in engineering, natural sciences, and social sciences were the least likely.[15]

Women were more likely than men to spend time on teaching in fall term 1992, and were less likely to have published (see Table 3.3).[16] Women produced slightly smaller numbers of student contact hours as men but made considerably more use of collaborative instructional techniques.[17]

Minority faculty were less likely than nonminority faculty to use collaborative instructional approaches. They produced fewer total student contact hours but on average published more.[18] Publishing increased with rank whereas time spent on teaching decreased with it.[19]

Table 3.2 Distribution of Group-Defining Variables, by Discipline Area

Discipline Area	Publishing, 2-Year		Total Instructional Productivity		Time Spent (%) Teaching		Collaborative Instruction Ratio	
	Mean	SE[a]	Mean	SE	Mean	SE	Mean	SE
Agriculture/Home Economics	4.76	.363	244.59	20.187	43.19	2.443	0.10	.024
Business	2.78	.166	292.21	8.432	53.00	.972	0.14	.014
Education	2.70	.160	275.46	16.611	56.23	.919	0.35	.017
Engineering	4.75	.301	223.79	12.539	48.89	1.140	0.018	.006
Fine Arts	1.38	.140	245.23	11.114	56.60	1.006	0.37	.020
Health Sciences	5.49	.256	533.93	34.134	41.03	.966	0.17	.014
Humanities	3.46	.126	252.55	5.804	59.25	.608	0.27	.011
Natural Sciences	4.94	.188	382.10	13.681	50.10	.702	0.05	.006
Social Sciences	3.94	.144	304.72	9.281	51.69	.717	0.08	.008
Other Areas	2.87	.131	304.13	11.828	54.64	.822	0.18	.013

Source: Adapted from NSOPF 1993.   [a] SE = Standard error

Table 3.3 Distribution of Group-Defining Variables, by Gender, Race/Ethnicity, and Academic Rank

	Publishing, 2-Year		Total Instructional Productivity		Time Spent (%), Teaching		Collaborative Instruction Ratio	
	Mean	SE[a]	Mean	SE	Mean	SE	Mean	SE
Gender								
Female	2.82	.086	293.04	7.328	56.58	.499	0.22	.008
Male	4.23	.081	333.14	6.495	50.04	.346	0.14	.005
Race/Ethnicity								
Nonminority	3.83	.070	328.08	5.655	51.48	.321	0.17	.004
Minority	4.29	.161	288.28	11.702	52.75	.631	0.13	.008
Academic Rank								
Professor	5.02	.130	331.26	9.391	48.81	.463	0.16	.007
Associate Professor	3.37	.093	326.10	8.077	51.82	.509	0.16	.007
Assistant Professor	2.95	.080	306.78	8.669	54.76	.529	0.17	.008
Instructor/Lecturer	1.32	.203	340.70	30.34	60.77	1.975	0.20	.028

Source: Adapted from NSOPF 1993.   [a] SE =Standard error

Tables 3.4, 3.5, and 3.6 present the distribution of the collaborative instruction ratio in more detail. More than three-fourths of all faculty members did *not* use a collaborative approach as the primary instructional technique in any of their courses during fall term 1992. About 9 percent used a collaborative technique in some of their classes, and about 14 percent used this approach in the majority of their classes. By program area, the percentage of faculty who claimed *not* to use a collaborative approach as the primary instructional method in any of their courses ranged from a high of about 97 percent in engineering to a low of about 49 percent in fine arts. This percentage did not vary substantially by gender, race/ethnicity, or academic rank.

Table 3.4 Frequency Distribution of Collaborative Instruction Ratio, by Type of Institution

Type of Institution	Collaborative Instruction Ratio			
	0	.01–.50	.51–1.00	Total
All 4-Year	77.2%	8.9%	13.9%	100%
Research	83.5%	4.5%	12.0%	100%
Doctoral	79.9%	7.7%	12.4%	100%
Comprehensive	72.0%	12.8%	15.2%	100%
Liberal Arts	68.4%	13.4%	18.2%	100%
Other 4-Year	81.6%	5.1%	13.3%	100%

Source: Adapted from NSOPF 1993.

Table 3.5 Frequency Distribution of Collaborative Instruction Ratio, by Discipline Area

Discipline Area	Collaborative Instruction Ratio			
	0	.01–.50	.51–1.00	Total
Agriculture/Home Economics	82.6%	10.8%	6.6%	100%
Business	80.1%	8.9%	11.0%	100%
Education	52.6%	15.5%	31.9%	100%
Engineering	96.8%	2.1%	1.1%	100%
Fine Arts	49.2%	18.7%	32.1%	100%
Health Sciences	76.7%	7.9%	15.4%	100%
Humanities	65.3%	10.7%	24.0%	100%
Natural Sciences	91.7%	4.1%	4.2%	100%
Social Sciences	87.6%	6.3%	6.1%	100%
Other Areas	73.1%	12.8%	14.1%	100%

Source: Adapted from NSOPF 1993.

Table 3.6 Frequency Distribution of Collaborative Instruction Ratio, by Gender, Race/Ethnicity, and Academic Rank

Discipline Area	Collaborative Instruction Ratio			
	0	.01-.50	.51-1.00	Total
Female	69.3%	10.9%	19.8%	100%
Male	79.8%	8.2%	12.0%	100%
Race/Ethnicity				
Non-minority	76.7%	9.1%	14.2%	100%
Minority	81.5%	7.3%	11.2%	100%
Academic Rank				
Professor	78.5%	8.8%	13.5%	100%
Associate Professor	77.7%	8.8%	13.5%	100%
Assistant Professor	75.1%	10.3%	14.6%	100%
Instructor/Lecturer	72.4%	8.7%	18.9%	100%

Source: Adapted from NSOPF 1993.

Research Question 2: What percentage of the faculty are productive in teaching and research?

Table 3.7 shows the percentage of faculty who fit the three definitions of "highly productive" teacher-researchers. About 10 percent of all faculty are above average (by discipline and type of institution) in both publishing and total instructional productivity (Group 1). This percentage does not vary significantly by type of institution. About 13 percent of faculty in four-year institutions are above average in both publishing productivity and in time spent on teaching (Group 2). Again, this percentage does not vary significantly by type of institution.

Finally, about 7 percent of faculty in four-year institutions are above average in publishing productivity and use collaborative instruction in their classroom teaching (Group 3). This percentage does not vary significantly by type of institution.

Table 3.7 Percentage of Faculty in High Performing Productivity Groups, by Type of Institution

Type of Institution	Group 1 Teaching Productivity and Research Productivity		Group 2 Teaching Time and Research Productivity		Group 3 Collaborative Instruction and Research Productivity	
	%	SE[a]	%	SE	%	SE
All 4-Year	10.47%	.36%	12.50%	.38%	7.11%	.31%
Research	9.94%	.83%	12.58%	.89%	5.34%	.64%
Doctoral	9.03%	.75%	12.68%	.86%	5.70%	.62%
Comprehensive	11.15%	.54%	12.31%	.57%	9.08%	.51%
Liberal Arts	11.01%	1.12%	13.24%	1.21%	7.69%	.97%
Other 4-Year	12.45%	1.65%	11.67%	1.47%	7.51%	1.34%

Source: Adapted from NSOPF 1993.
[a] SE = standard error

Table 3.8 shows the same distributions by program area; Table 3.9 presents the results by gender, race/ethnicity, and academic rank. Although membership in Group 1 did not vary by discipline and few differences existed for Group 2 (faculty in health sciences were less likely to achieve Group 2),[20] membership in Group 3 varied substantially by discipline. Faculty in education and the humanities were more likely to attain Group 3 status, whereas faculty in engineering, natural sciences, and social sciences were less likely to do so.[21] This finding parallels the similar variation in the use of collaborative instructional techniques by academic discipline.

Women were less likely to attain Group 1 status, more likely to attain Group 3.[22] Minority faculty were less likely than nonminority faculty to attain Group 1, more likely to attain Group 2.[23] By academic rank, the most interesting finding is that professors and *assistant* professors were more likely to attain Group 2 status than either associate professors or lecturers.[24]

Table 3.8 Percentage of Faculty in High Performing Productivity Groups, by Discipline Area

Type of Institution	Group 1 Teaching Productivity and Research Productivity		Group 2 Teaching Time and Research Productivity		Group 3 Collaborative Instruction and Research Productivity	
	%	SE[a]	%	SE	%	SE
Agriculture/ Home Economics	7.38%	2.35%	11.12%	2.59%	3.19%	1.65%
Business	12.59%	1.45%	13.34%	1.49%	6.53%	1.11%
Education	9.28%	1.15%	13.81%	1.37%	18.23%	1.57%
Engineering	7.85%	1.40%	12.63%	1.73%	0.89%	.51%
Fine Arts	8.94%	1.32%	11.17%	1.45%	10.06%	1.43%
Health Sciences	9.48%	1.17%	8.85%	1.03%	6.29%	1.00%
Humanities	11.07%	.84%	13.99%	.93%	10.01%	.83%
Natural Sciences	8.96%	.77%	11.44%	.85%	3.01%	.47%
Social Sciences	12.74%	1.07%	13.09%	1.08%	4.90%	.71%
Other Areas	13.49%	1.26%	16.31%	1.36%	9.05%	1.08%

Source: Adapted from NSOPF 1993.
[a] SE = standard error

Table 3.9 Percentage of Faculty in High Performing Productivity Groups, by Gender, Race/Ethnicity, and Academic Rank

	Group 1 Teaching Productivity and Research Productivity		Group 2 Teaching Time and Research Productivity		Group 3 Collaborative Instruction and Research Productivity	
	%	SE[a]	%	SE	%	SE
Gender						
Female	8.85%	.58%	12.93%	.68%	9.11%	.61%
Male	11.00%	.45%	12.36%	.46%	6.46%	.36%
Race/Ethnicity						
Nonminority	10.72%	.41%	12.23%	.42%	7.24%	.35%
Minority	8.70%	.74%	14.48%	.90%	6.10%	.65%
Academic Rank						
Professor	11.89%	.62%	13.22%	.64%	7.73%	.53%
Associate Professor	9.71%	.62%	10.84%	.64%	6.56%	.54%
Assistant Professor	9.56%	.64%	13.69%	.73%	7.23%	.58%
Instructor/ Lecturer	6.08%	1.77%	8.51%	2.04%	1.60%	.96%

Source: Adapted from NSOPF 1993.
[a] SE = standard error

Research Question 3: What distinguishes faculty members who are highly productive in teaching and research from their less productive colleagues?

To identify the characteristics and experiences that distinguish faculty who meet the *complete faculty member* profile from their counterparts, I regressed group membership (i.e., either a member of Group 1 or not) on the variables shown in Figure 3.1 separately by type of institution.[25] Although several controls (institutional size and wealth, academic discipline, and personal characteristics) are included in the analyses and shown in the tables, this discussion focuses on the theoretical constructs described previously—early socialization, current socialization/self-motivation, work allocation, departmental climate and resources, rewards, and other measures of productivity. Table 3.10 presents the logistic regression results, by type of institution. Table 3.11 summarizes the logistic regression results.

Table 3.10 Logistic Regression Model for Teaching/Research Productivity Group 1,[a] by Type of Institution

	Research	Doctoral	Comprehensive	Liberal Arts	Other
$-2 \log L^{bc}$	105.178, 34 df	111.958, 34 df	256.262, 34 df	56.935, 29 df	59.101, 27 df
Concordant	77.7%	76.9%	77.0%	73.9%	81.1%
Discordant	21.9%	22.4%	22.4%	25.7%	18.2%
Tied	.4%	.7%	.6%	.4%	.7%
Somers D	.558	.545	.545	.483	.630
Indicators	Parameters	Parameters	Parameters	Parameters	Parameters
Intercept	-21.8112***	-6.3960	-10.2967*	-5.3145	2.8932
Controls					
Institution					
FTE Enrollment (School Size)	0.000014	-0.00002	0.000114***	0.000088	-0.00052

Education and General Expenditures	-629E-13	6.901E-9**	-6.92E-9*	-3.56E-9	4.081E-9
Discipline					
Agriculture/Home Economics	-1.509	-2.332*	-.885	N/A	N/A
Business	.235	.475	.009	N/A	N/A
Education	-2.223*	-.164	-.208	N/A	N/A
Engineering	-1.132	-2.216**	.156	N/A	N/A
Fine Arts	-.600	-2.040*	-.372	-.753	N/A
Health Sciences	-1.135	-2.344**	-.281	N/A	.238
Humanities	.061	.014	.048	-.185	N/A
Natural Science	-.670	-1.625*	-.889***	-.374	-.908
Social Science	-.158	-.699	-.209	-.220	N/A

(continued next page)

Table 3.10 *(continued)*

Controls *(continued)*	Research	Doctoral	Comprehensive	Liberal Arts	Other
Personal					
Gender	-.001	.918	-.143	.943**	-1.477*
Race/Ethnicity	-.078	-.419	-.404	.464	-3.077
Academic Rank	.108	.214	.220*	-.314	-1.039*
Early Socialization					
Teaching Assistantship	.140	.027	.357*	.126	.705
Holds Doctorate or Equivalent	-.069	.069	.231*	.237	.717
Previous college teaching experience	.289	.110	.140	.627*	-.229
Previous college research experience	-.281	.676	.495	.675	-2.745*

Current Socialization/ Self-motivation					
Teaching					
If respondent left present institution, importance of no pressure to publish	-.778***	-.188	-.456***	-.168	-.938*
Research					
Agree that research/publication should be primary criterion for P/T	.283	.382**	.228**	.213	.264
If respondent left present institution, importance of good research facilities	.459	-.204	.180	.553*	-.465

(continued next page)

Table 3.10 (continued)

	Research	Doctoral	Comprehensive	Liberal Arts	Other
Work Allocation					
Hours in Class per Week	.085	.085***	.076***	.070***	.029
Taught Only Graduate Students	-1.362*	-1.363***	-1.145***	.965	.600
Is Department Chair	-1.602**	-.061	-.309	-.161	-.591
Climate/Resources					
Satisfied with Authority to Choose Classes to Teach	-.123	.308	-.134	.174	-.670
Adequacy of Personal Computers at Institution	.339*	-.220	-.052	-.122	-.802*
Adequacy of University Library Facilities	.379*	-.049	.122	-.029	-.137

Rewards					
At this institution, research is rewarded more than teaching	.394*	-.235	-.179**	-.204	-.186
Basic Salary (log)	1.342*	.237	.595	.064	.459
Productivity Predictors					
Research					
Number of Grants on Which Respondent Was PI or Co-PI	.196	.534***	.270*	.693**	1.367***
Number of Presentations at Conferences	.010	.042***	.042*	.007	.028

(continued next page)

Table 3.10 *(continued)*

Productivity Predictors *(continued)*	Research	Doctoral	Comprehensive	Liberal Arts	Other
Teaching					
Student Contact Hours	N/A	N/A	N/A	N/A	N/A
Independent Study Contact Hours Per Week	N/A	N/A	N/A	N/A	N/A
Number of Thesis or Dissertation Committees Served On	.023*	.026	.029***	.041	-.055
Productivity-Related Criteria					
Research					
Number of Refereed Publications during Previous Two Years [d]	N/A	N/A	N/A	N/A	N/A

Teaching				
Total Instructional Productivity [e]	N/A	N/A	N/A	N/A	N/A
Time Allocation				
More Time on Research, Less on Teaching [f]	-.003	.006	.0005	-.004	.004
Instructional Approach				
Ratio of Collaborative Instruction as Primary Teaching Approach to Total number of Courses Taught	-.730	-1.878**	-.084	.695	.380

Source: Adapted from NSOPF 1993.

[a] Group 1 = above the norm in total instructional productivity and refereed publications during the previous two years.

[b] -2 log L is based on unweighted number of respondents. Other measures of association are based on weighted respondents.

[c] All chi-square values are significant at $p < .001$.

[d] Refereed articles, published book reviews, books, monographs, chapters in edited books

[e] Student classroom contact hours plus independent study contact hours

[f] Percentage of time spent on research minus percentage of time spent on teaching

Table 3.11 Summary of Logistic Regression Results for Group 1,[a] by Type of Institution

	Research	Doctoral	Compre-hensive	Liberal Arts	Other
Early Socialization					
Teaching Assistantship			+[b]		
Holds Doctorate or Equivalent			+		
Previous College Teaching Experience				+	
Previous College Research Experience					-
Current Socialization/ Self-motivation					
Teaching					
If respondent left present institution, importance of no pressure to publish	- - -		- - -		-
Research					
Agree that research/publication should be primary criterion for P/T		++	++		
If respondent left present institution, importance of good research facilities				+	

Table 3.11 *(continued)*

	Research	Doctoral	Compre- hensive	Liberal Arts	Other
Work Allocation					
Hours in Class per Week	+++	+++	+++	+++	
Taught Only Graduate Students	- - -	- - -	- - -		
Is Department Chair	- -				
Climate/Resources					
Satisfied with Authority to Choose Classes to Teach					
Adequacy of Personal Computers at Institution	+				-
Adequacy of University Library Facilities	+				
Rewards					
At this institution, research is rewarded more than teaching	+		- -		
Basic Salary (log)	+				

Table 3.11 *(continued)*

	Research	Doctoral	Compre-hensive	Liberal Arts	Other
Productivity Predictors					
Research					
Number of Grants on Which Respondent Was PI or Co-PI		+++	+	++	+++
Number of Presentations at Conferences		+++	+		
Teaching					
Student Contact Hours	N/A	N/A	N/A	N/A	N/A
Independent Study Contact Hours per Week	N/A	N/A	N/A	N/A	N/A
Number of Thesis or Dissertation Committees Served On	+		+++		
Productivity-Related Criteria					
Research					
Number of Refereed Publications during Previous Two Years [c]	N/A	N/A	N/A	N/A	N/A
Teaching					
Total Instructional Productivity [d]	N/A	N/A	N/A	N/A	N/A

Table 3.11 *(continued)*

	Research	Doctoral	Comprehensive	Liberal Arts	Other
Time Allocation					
More Time on Research, Less on Teaching [e]					
Instructional Approach					
Ratio of Collaborative Instruction as Primary Teaching Approach to Total Number of Courses Taught		- -			

Source: Adapted from NSOPF 1993.

[a] Group 1 = above the norm in total instructional productivity and refereed publications during previous two years

[b] + = positively related, $p < .05$ - = negatively related, $p < .05$
++ = positively related, $p < .01$ -- = negatively related, $p < .01$
+++ = positively related, $p < .001$ --- = negatively related, $p < .001$

[c] Refereed articles, published book reviews, books, monographs, chapters in edited books

[d] Student classroom contact hours plus independent study contact hours

[e] Percentage of time spent on research minus percentage of time spent on teaching

Research Universities

None of the measures of early socialization were significantly related to group membership. Faculty in Group 1 were significantly less likely to say that they would leave because of publishing pressure, a measure of current socialization/self-motivation. Work allocation was strongly related to group membership—faculty who spent more hours in the classroom, who taught both undergraduate and graduate students, and who were not assigned major administrative duties were more likely to achieve above average publishing and instructional productivity. Both resources and rewards were modestly related to group membership. Faculty in Group 1 were more likely to feel that their access to personal computers and the quality of library holdings were adequate. Faculty in Group 1 were more likely to agree that research was rewarded more than teaching at their institutions and to receive higher salaries.

Doctorate-Granting Universities

Early socialization is unrelated to group membership. One measure of current socialization—agreement that research productivity should be the primary criterion for promotion and tenure—is positively related to group membership. Faculty in Group 1 who spent more hours in class per week and who taught both undergraduate and graduate—both measures of work allocation—were more likely to achieve high productivity in teaching and research. Neither departmental climate and resources nor rewards were related to group membership. Obtaining funded research projects and giving presentations, both measures of research productivity, were positively related to group membership. Faculty who made extensive use of collaborative instructional techniques were less likely to achieve above average productivity in both teaching and research. Since collaborative instructional approaches are more labor-intensive than traditional lectures and seminars, it seems that spending more hours teaching in a traditional style is less likely to consume more time overall (i.e., percentage of time spent on teaching) than the use of collaborative instructional approaches.

Comprehensive Colleges and Universities

In contrast to research-oriented institutions, in comprehensives early socialization is related to group membership—high producing teacher-researchers were more likely to have been a teaching assistant in graduate school and to obtain a doctorate from a major research university. Current socialization also mattered: agreeing with research productivity as the primary criterion in promotion and tenure and not desiring to escape pressures to publish are positively related to group membership. As with research-oriented institutions, hours spent in class per week and type of students taught—both measures of work allocation—affect productivity. Faculty in Group 1 were more likely to be on dissertation and thesis committees, a measure of teaching productivity. At the same time, they were more likely to give conference presentations and obtain grants. Faculty in Group 1 were less likely to perceive that research is rewarded more than teaching at their institutions.

Liberal Arts Colleges

One measure of early socialization—previous college teaching experience—is positively related to teaching and research productivity. Highly productive faculty in liberal arts colleges were more likely to say that they would leave to find better research facilities (current socialization/self-motivation). They were also more likely to spend more hours in the classroom and to obtain external research funds.

Other Four-Year Institutions

Faculty in Group 1 were less likely to have had previous collegiate research employment (early socialization), less likely to seek employment characterized by less pressure to publish (self-motivation), less likely to be satisfied with personal computer resources (climate/ resources), and more likely to have obtained external research funding (research productivity).

DISCUSSION

The small percentage of faculty in all types of four-year institutions who achieved above average levels of output in both research and teaching (regardless of definition) belies the common belief that each faculty member can achieve both simultaneously. Despite personnel policies for tenure-track faculty that presume simultaneous productivity in research and teaching, staffing patterns reflect the difficulty in achieving such a mix. Gappa and Leslie (1993) demonstrate that four-year colleges and universities increasingly rely on part-time and adjunct faculty and teaching assistants to attain acceptable levels of instructional productivity, thereby freeing time for full-time faculty to focus on research.

Achieving teaching and research productivity in *research universities* requires four ingredients. First, achieving high levels of teaching productivity requires that faculty work assignments run counter to institutional norms—teaching more hours in class per week and not limiting instruction to graduate students. Second, adequate resources for research—personal computers and libraries—must also be available. Third, faculty members' *perceptions* of rewards should be consistent with research, but the *actual* rewards (compensation) must reinforce achieving teaching productivity as well as research output. Finally, faculty members in research universities who feel that their fit with the publishing focus of the institution is a good one are more likely to achieve high levels of teaching and research productivity.

Simultaneously achieving high levels of teaching and research productivity in *doctorate-granting universities* appears to require three conditions: (1) the work assignment must emphasize instructional productivity—greater hours in the classroom (although this work assignment comes at the cost of making it more difficult to use innovative instructional approaches); (2) high levels of other types of research productivity must be attained; and (3) the individual faculty member must believe in the importance of research.

The keys to simultaneously publishing and generating student contact hours in *comprehensive colleges and universities* appear to be (a) a work assignment that emphasizes classroom instruction, (b) productivity in all aspects of teaching and research, (c) faculty attitudes about the value of research in promotion and tenure, and (d) a perception that research is not rewarded more than teaching at the institution (i.e., believing that spending time on teaching will not harm the faculty member's career).

The strongest predictor of teaching and research productivity for faculty in *liberal arts colleges* is work assignment—spending more hours teaching in the classroom. Previous teaching experience, an indicator most likely consistent with teaching productivity, is positively related to being productive in teaching and research. On the research side, obtaining research moneys, a measure of research productivity, and considering changing jobs to find better research facilities are indicative of teaching and research productivity. Finally, by far the strongest indicator of simultaneously publishing and generating student contact hours for faculty in *other four-year institutions* is another measure of research productivity, obtaining funded research projects.

POLICY IMPLICATIONS

To encourage high productivity in both teaching and research, specific institutional policies and practices and individual preferences apparently must simultaneously reinforce either teaching or research productivity,[26] often in ways counter to dominant norms. Across all types of four-year institutions, the most common factor in simultaneously achieving high teaching and research productivity is to spend more hours in the classroom. However, this effort may deter faculty members from using collaborative teaching techniques. Faculty with higher classroom work assignments typically are able to publish at greater than average rates because they also have research grants, which gives them the opportunity to publish from their ongoing research work. Although not included in this study, availability of teaching assistants may permit faculty members to teach large undergraduate classes with a relatively modest investment in time. Faculty attitudes and beliefs are also important, especially the fit with institutional missions and the perception that research should be the primary criterion in promotion and tenure. The latter indicator is particularly important for faculty in comprehensive colleges and universities where such a belief may be counter to institutional norms.

These results help explain why so few faculty are able to achieve above average levels of teaching and research productivity at the same time. Few faculty are able to publish while carrying above average teaching loads. Few faculty members have externally funded research projects, a resource that increases their ability to publish while teaching above average numbers of students. These results also help clarify the roles of faculty attitudes and beliefs in overall productivity. When confronted with a substantial classroom work assignment and the desire (or pressure) to publish, the deciding factor may be the faculty member's own beliefs about the importance of research or teaching.

These results strongly suggest that the faculty member who simultaneously achieves above average levels of productivity in teaching and research—the *complete faculty member*—is rare. For most faculty, generating high numbers of student contact hours diminishes publication rates, and vice versa. Descriptive data suggest that the same applies to spending a large percentage of time on teaching or using labor-intensive collaborative instruction techniques—it is the exceptional faculty member (and not many of them), not the average one, who achieves these instructional outputs while publishing at an above average rate.

For most departments, the key to increasing teaching and research productivity may lie in looking for group solutions rather than in relying on each faculty member simultaneously to increase productivity levels in teaching and research. Viewing faculty productivity as an aggregate across faculty members permits department chairs and departmental committees to combine the efforts of their individual members to achieve acceptable levels of productivity. Faculty who are less productive in research can increase the departmental average in teaching productivity, whereas faculty who publish extensively can contribute to aggregate research productivity goals. In any case, the departmental or aggregate view of faculty productivity implies far more interdependence than is currently accepted as the norm for faculty behavior.

NOTES

1. Population estimates from survey data were based on weights derived from the inverse of the probability of a faculty member in a particular type of institution being selected. The probability of selecting a faculty member for the sample was a function of the odds of an institution being selected from the universe of accredited postsecondary institutions and the probability of a faculty member being selected from the population within his or her institution. Imputed data were replaced with missing values, which accounts for the difference between the number of eligible respondents and the actual cases used in the logistic regression analyses.

2. Limiting the time period for the measure of research productivity to the preceding two years was necessary to compare it with teaching workloads and productivity during fall term 1992. Although Hattie and Marsh (1996) argue that weighted scales for publishing productivity may be preferable to simple numbers of publications, selecting weights that are applicable across disciplines and types of institutions is impractical and can be misleading. For example, a book may be valued more highly in history whereas a refereed article in a top journal may be valued more highly in engineering. For this reason, I estimated number of publications with a simple count of eligible publications.

3. *Student classroom contact hours per week* equals the number of hours the faculty member taught in a specific class per week times the number of students enrolled in that class, summed over all the classes taught during fall term 1992. *Independent study contact hours per week* is the faculty members estimated number of additional contact hours with students taking independent study courses with him or her during fall term 1992. Although few authors have used total instructional productivity in their research, many have used *hours in the classroom per week* (e.g., Bayer, 1973; Fulton and Trow, 1974) and *student classroom contact hours* (e.g., Fairweather, 1996).

4. As a primary instructional approach, *NSOPF 1993* defined "seminar" and "discussion group and class presentations" separately. The latter type clearly fit the definition of collaborative instruction, whereas the former did not.

5. The measure focuses on the primary instructional technique used in each class. Although faculty members relying primarily on lectures for a specific class could have included some collaborative learning activities, I coded the class as using a noncollaborative technique since the primary instructional approach was lecturing.

6. Groups 1, 2, and 3 are not mutually exclusive.

7. Academic discipline was defined according to 10 program areas: agriculture/home economics, business, education, engineering, fine arts, health sciences, humanities, natural sciences, social sciences, and other fields. In the logistic regression analyses, the number of program areas was reduced to five for liberal arts colleges (fine arts, humanities, natural sciences, social sciences, and other fields) and three for other four-year institutions (health sciences, natural sciences, other fields) because of the limited variation in some program areas.

8. t (res/doc) = 9.50***; t(res/oth) = 2.92***; t(oth/doc) = 3.20**; t(doc/comp) = 13.58***; t(comp/lib) = 2.82** where * = p < .05, ** = p < .01, *** = p < .005. The comparison being made is shown in parentheses. For this analysis, the comparison is based on caneyie type. t(res/doc) refers to the mean difference between the publications rate of faculty members in research universities with faculty members in doctoral-granting universities. t(res/oth) refers to research and other 4-year institutions. Only significant t-test results are shown.

9. t(res/lib) = 4.00***; t(doc/lib) = 5.47***; t(comp/lib) = 8.22***; t(oth/res) = 4.85***; t(oth/doc) = 4.58***; t(oth/lib) = 7.07***.

10. t(res/doc) = -12.15***; t(doc/comp) = -7.94***; t(comp/lib) = -6.31***.

11. t(doc/comp) = 3.15**.

12. t(business) = -6.24***; t(education) = -6.92***; t(engineering) = 2.79*; t(fine arts) = -16.30***; t(health sciences) = 6.06***; t(humanities) = -3.05*; t(natural sciences) = 5.30***; t(other) = -7.03***. For academic disciplines, t tests were based on comparing the mean for the program area with the overall mean. Bonferroni corrections were used to estimate the level of significance of each test.

13. t(health sciences) = 6.10***; t(natural sciences) = 4.03***; t(agriculture) = -3.78***; t(business) = -3.16*; t(education) = -2.75*; t(engineering) = -7.36***; t(fine arts) = -6.39***; t(humanities) = -5.78***.

14. t(education) = 4.77***; t(fine arts) = 4.73***; t(humanities) = 11.34***; t(other) = 3.46**; t(agriculture) = -3.43**; t(health sciences) = -10.43***.

15. t(education) = 10.86***; t(fine arts) = 10.50***; t(humanities) = 9.40***; t(engineering) = -19.44***; t(natural sciences) = -13.89***; t(social sciences) = -8.89***.

16. t(publishing) = -2.02*; t(% teaching) = 10.72***.

17. t(student contact hours) = -2.14*; t(collaborative) = 8.51***.

18. t(publishing) = 2.61**; t(student contact hours) = -3.08**; t(collaborative) = -4.44***.

19. Publishing: t(prof/assoc) = 10.31***; t(assoc/asst) = 3.43***; t(asst/lect) = 7.41***. Time spent on teaching: t(prof/assoc) = -4.38**; t(assoc/asst) = -4.01***; t(asst/lect) = -2.95**.

20. Group 2: t(health sciences) = -3.32***; t(other) = 2.70**.

21. t(education) = 6.95***; t(humanities) = 3.27**; t(engineering) = -10.37***; t(natural sciences) = -7.32***; t(social sciences) = -2.85*.

22. t(Group 1) = -2.93**; t(Group 3) = 3.73***.

23. t(Group 1) = -2.38*; t(Group 2) = 1.97*.

24. Group 1: t(prof/assoc) = 2.83**. Group 2: t(prof/assoc) = 2.63**; t(asst/assoc) = 2.94**; t(prof/lect) = 2.20*; t(asst/lect) = 2.39*. Group 3: t(asst/lect) = 4.51***.

25. Throughout the discussion, the phrase "group membership" refers to whether or not a faculty member was a member of Group 1.

26. Rarely will a single policy or specific attribute reinforce both teaching and research productivity at the same time.

REFERENCES

Alpert, D. (1985). Performance and paralysis: The organizational context of the American research university. *Journal of Higher Education, 56,* 241–281.

Ashby, E. (1974). *Adapting universities to a technological society.* San Francisco: Jossey-Bass.

Austin, A.E. (1992). Supporting junior faculty through a teaching fellows program. In M.D. Sorcinelli and A.E. Austin (Eds.), *Developing new and junior faculty* (pp. 73–86). New Directions for Teaching and Learning, No. 50. San Francisco: Jossey-Bass.

Baldridge, J.V., Curtis, D., Ecker, G., and Riley, G. (1978). *Policy making and effective leadership.* San Francisco: Jossey-Bass.

Baldwin, R.G., and Blackburn, R.T. (1981). The academic career as a developmental process. *Journal of Higher Education, 52,* 598–614.

Bayer, A.E. (1973). Teaching faculty in academe: 1972–1973. *ACE Research Reports, 8,* 1–68.

Bess, J.L. (1978). Anticipatory socialization of graduate students. *Research in Higher Education, 8,* 289–317.

Blackburn, R.T., and Lawrence, J.H. (1995). *Faculty at work: Motivation, expectation, satisfaction.* Baltimore, MD: Johns Hopkins University Press.

Bland, C.J., and Schmitz, C.C. (1986). Characteristics of the successful researcher and implications for faculty development. *Journal of Medical Education, 61,* 22–31.

Boice, R. (1992). *The new faculty member.* San Francisco: Jossey-Bass.

Bok, D. (1992). Reclaiming the public trust. *Change, 24,* 12–19.

Bruffee, K.A. (1993). *Collaborative learning: Higher education, interdependence, and the authority of knowledge.* Baltimore, MD: Johns Hopkins University Press.

Carnegie Foundation for the Advancement of Teaching. (1987). *A classification of institutions of higher education.* Princeton, NJ:

Clark, B.R. (1963). Faculty organization and authority. In T.F. Lunsford (Ed.), *The study of academic administration* (pp. 37–51). Boulder, CO: Western Interstate Commission on Higher Education.

————. (1972). The organizational saga in higher education. *Administrative Science Quarterly, 17,* 178–184.

————. (1987). *The academic life: Small worlds, different worlds.* Princeton, NJ: Carnegie Foundation for the Advancement of Teaching.

Clark, S.M., and Corcoran, M. (1986). Perspectives on the professional socialization of women faculty. *Journal of Higher Education, 57,* 20–43.

Colbeck, C. (April, 1997). *The main reciprocal of teaching load: Faculty use of research time.* Paper presented at the annual meeting of the American Educational Research Association, Chicago.

Crimmel, H. (1984). The myth of the teacher-scholar. *Liberal Education, 70,* 183–198.

Diamond, R.M. (1993). Changing priorities in the faculty reward system. In R.M. Diamond and B.E. Adam (Eds.), *Recognizing faculty work: Reward systems for the year 2000* (pp. 5–12). New Directions for Higher Education, No. 81. San Francisco: Jossey-Bass.

Fairweather, J.S. (1993). Faculty rewards reconsidered: The nature of tradeoffs. *Change, 25,* 44–47.

————. (1996). *Faculty work and public trust: Restoring the value of teaching and public service in American academic life.* Boston: Allyn and Bacon.

Fairweather, J.S., and Rhoads, R.A. (1995). Teaching and the faculty role: Enhancing the commitment to instruction in American colleges and universities. *Education Evaluation and Policy Analysis, 17,* 179–194.

Feldman, K.A. (1987). Research productivity and scholarly accomplishment of college teachers as related to their instructional effectiveness: A review and exploration. *Research in Higher Education, 26,* 227–298.

Finkelstein, M.J. (1984). *The American academic profession: A synthesis of social science inquiry since World War II.* Columbus, OH: Ohio State University Press.

Fulton, O., and Trow, M. (1974). Research activity in American higher education. *Sociology of Education, 47,* 29–73.

Gappa, J.M., and Leslie, D.W. (1993). *The invisible faculty: Improving the status of part-timers in higher education.* San Francisco: Jossey-Bass.

Geiger, R.L. (1986). *To advance knowledge: The growth of American research universities, 1900–1940.* New York: Oxford University Press.

Goodsell, A.S., Maher, M., and Tinto V.(1992). *Collaborative learning: A source book for higher education.* University Park, PA: National Center on Postsecondary Teaching, Learning, and Assessment.

Hattie, J., and Marsh, H.W. (1996). The relationship between research and teaching: A meta-analysis. *Review of Educational Research, 66,* 507–542.

Johnstone, D.B. (1993). The cost of higher education: Worldwide issues and trends for the 1990s. In P.G. Altbach and D.B. Johnstone (Eds.), *The funding of higher education: International perspectives* (3–24). New York: Garland.

Konrad, A.M., and Pfeffer, J. (1990). Do you get what you deserve? Factors affecting the relationship between productivity and pay. *Administrative Science Quarterly, 35,* 258–285.

Ladd, E.C., Jr. (1979). The work experience of American college professors: Some data and an argument. In *Current issues in higher education.* Washington, DC: American Association of Higher Education.

Linsky, A.S., and Straus, M. (1975). Student evaluation, research productivity, and eminence of college faculty. *Journal of Higher Education, 46,* 89–102.

Massy, W., and Wilger, A. (1995). Improving productivity: What faculty think about it—and its effect on quality. *Change, 27,* 10–21.

Reynolds, A. (1992). Charting the changes in junior faculty: Relationships among socialization, acculturation, and gender. *Journal of Higher Education, 63,* 637–652.

Weimer, M. (1990). *Improving college teaching: Strategies for developing instructional effectiveness.* San Francisco: Jossey-Bass.

———. (1996). *Teaching on solid ground: Using scholarship to improve teaching.* San Francisco: Jossey-Bass.

CHAPTER 4

Documenting Diversity
The Professional Portfolio and Faculty Rewards

Robert M. Diamond
Bronwyn E. Adam

Faculty are different from one another in many ways. They have different strengths, interests, and personal histories and are shaped differently by the institutions at which they work, the assignments they are given, and their academic disciplines and the areas of specialization within them. In an ideal situation, the promotion and tenure process—the basis for the faculty reward system—would be sensitive to these differential factors and would consider faculty candidates within their unique institutional and departmental contexts. Unfortunately, this is not typically the case. Narrow, exclusive definitions of scholarship constrain faculty vitality and creativity, counter the stated priorities and missions of colleges and universities, and prevent many faculty from making important contributions to their campuses and larger communities.

In this chapter we will address the need for an inclusive faculty reward system—one that recognizes and values the full range of contributions made by faculty to their institutions, communities, and disciplines. We will focus on three areas: (1) defining faculty work—with particular emphasis on institutional and disciplinary differences; (2) documenting the full range of faculty work; and (3) assessment—the process of evaluating the quality and significance of faculty work. We will argue for a faculty reward system that supports faculty inquiry, innovation, and invention as it recognizes the unique contributions made by individuals in particular contexts.

DEFINING FACULTY WORK

While individuals have personal strengths and interests, two important external factors affect most significantly what faculty do—their institution and their academic discipline. Faculty in liberal arts colleges are called upon to enact different faculty roles than faculty in research universities, and education professors or those in the professional schools may make scholarly contributions that appear quite different from those made by colleagues in the natural and social sciences. Unfortunately, traditional faculty reward systems have not honored these powerful and dynamic differences. Rather, the system has applied a one-size-fits-all model to the assessment and reward of faculty work. This approach has hampered institutions' efforts to meet their goals and has proven a disservice to many productive and committed faculty. It is time to recognize that faculty need models of different sizes and shapes to represent their unique contributions as teachers and scholars.

THE INSTITUTION

Institutional missions and priorities vary across and within institution types. Across the Carnegie Classifications from Research I to Baccalaureate (liberal arts) II institutions, institutional priorities emphasizing research, publication, and the garnering of grants shift to an emphasis on teaching and working in applied settings. A national survey of over 54,000 faculty, departmental chairs, and academic deans (Gray, Diamond and Adam, 1996) confirmed a shift in the relative importance of research and undergraduate teaching "from the research side of the continuum to the teaching side of the continuum when comparing graduate research institutions (Carnegie Research and Doctoral categories) to undergraduate teaching institutions (Carnegie Master's and Baccalaureate categories)" (p. 33). While fairly consistent, the continuum reflects variance at the level of the individual institution and at the level of particular institutional type. Variables such as institutional size and history, public or private status, and administrative leadership affect the degree to which mission and priorities are perceived similarly by members of the campus community.

Faculty at all types of institutions report performing a broad range of activities as part of their faculty role. If the faculty recognition and reward system is to be fair to faculty working in different contexts, it is important that the process be sensitive to the wide range of institutional factors that impact faculty and their work, including their differential assignments. Other factors affecting faculty work include national initiatives to focus greater attention on undergraduate teaching at research and doctoral institutions, greater faculty involvement in course and curriculum revision—especially around new technologies and pedagogies—and responsibility for student recruitment, advising, and retention.

Part of the customary faculty role includes serving on institutional and departmental committees. While some committee work is easily taken up, other assignments such as promotion and tenure, curriculum, or budget can easily assume a block of time over an extended period. Faculty are asked to serve as departmental chairs or to take up other administrative roles that are difficult and different from the roles they were prepared to assume as teacher—scholars. They may also be asked to undertake the restructuring of a curriculum, including design of new courses or redesign of existing ones. When such assignments are for a semester or longer (often the case with chairs, curriculum development, or work on externally funded projects), formally stopping the tenure clock or modifying the criteria for promotion and/or tenure are options that should be explored.

THE DISCIPLINE

While faculty assignments are made within an institutional context, faculty members' perceptions about the relative importance of the particular activities within their assignments are influenced, in part, by factors outside of the institution. In 1989 when Syracuse University began to explore ways to focus greater attention on the quality of students' undergraduate experience, two clear messages emerged from conversations with faculty. First, faculty priorities would not change until the institution's promotion and tenure system changed. Second, in order for the promotion and tenure process to change, faculty needed confidence that their national disciplinary associations would recognize an expanded range of scholarly or professional work for their fields. To address these challenges, a series of projects were launched at Syracuse, funded in part by the Fund for the Improvement of Postsecondary Education (FIPSE) and the Lilly Endowment, Inc., that provided funds to disciplinary associations so that they might develop statements describing the full range of faculty work in their fields. An important project goal was that these statements be descriptive, *not* prescriptive. The statements on scholarly work were careful to recognize the contexts within which they would be applied and to encourage academic departments to shape a priority system that was appropriate for their institutions.

The Modern Language Association's Commission on Professional Service, in the introduction to their document, *Making Faculty Work Visible: Reinterpreting Professional Service, Teaching, and Research in the Fields of Language and Literature* (1996), makes the following observations concerning the interrelationship of the discipline to individual and institutional priorities:

> In addition to these tensions between the research and the teaching mission of the university, recent years have seen a growing emphasis on its societal mission. As the sciences are asking themselves: What is the social responsibility of the scientist?, so are humanists starting to discuss: What are the social obligations of the humanist or of the scholar in the humanities? What is professional service in the fields of language and literature? Such questions are asked at a time when American colleges and universities are under increased economic pressure to produce and transmit knowledge that is of immediate and practical relevance to the job market. The demographic changes also exert pressure on institutions to diversify their criteria of excellence according to their stated mission and the diverse nature of their student body. The growth of academic technology produces new forms of knowledge and provides new forms of dissemination that require new forms of evaluation. It also generates a greater variety of applied work that does not fit within traditional disciplinary boundaries. Given the growing uncertainties of the job market, junior faculty want to maintain as great an autonomy as possible; they are keen on developing portable expertise that allows them to retain flexible career patterns with utmost geographic mobility; at the same time, however, institutions are defining their mission more sharply than before, and increasingly expect their faculty to serve their specific needs. (p. 7)

The special combination of forces and factors around each discipline and the uniqueness of each field make statements describing the scholarship of the disciplines important guides to assessing faculty work. While they serve the purpose of staking out the territory for scholarship within the field, they also serve to communicate these differences to faculty from other fields serving on promotion and tenure and other award and review committees.

The original plan for the Redefining Scholarly Work Project was to invite the participation of approximately six disciplines. Interest from disciplinary associations was so strong that funding was expanded to include some 30 disciplines. Seventeen groups completed statements by January 1997, and an additional 10 are in the process of completing documents in a second phase of the project. Participating associations include fields from the humanities, the social sciences, the natural sciences, the arts, and the professional fields, including:

*† American Academy of Religion
American Anthropological Association
*† American Assembly of Collegiate Schools of Business
*† American Chemical Society
American Educational Research Association
*† American Historical Association
American Philosophical Association
American Physical Society
American Political Science Association
American Psychological Association
American Society of Civil Engineers
† American Sociological Association
* Association of American Geographers
Association of American Medical Colleges
Association of College and Research Libraries
* Association for Education in Journalism and
    Mass Communication
* Council of Administrators of Family and Consumer Sciences
Council on Social Work Education
† Geological Society of America
* Joint Policy Board for Mathematics
† Modern Language Association
* National Office for Arts Accreditation in Higher Education
        (includes the fields of landscape architecture, architecture,
        art and design, dance, music, and theater)
Society for College Science Teachers

* Statements in *The Disciplines Speak* (Diamond and Adam, 1995)
† Statements completed

SOME OBSERVATIONS

The documents completed by the task force groups reflect common concerns and practices as well as important discipline—based differences. Authors of the statements, for example, shared frustration with the one-size-fits-all model that has historically been applied to considerations of faculty work. The differences in the statements reflect the very reasons why this model has not been a good fit for all disciplines or for all faculty. Each discipline identified problems with existing reward systems—problems that made it important that a statement describing the work of faculty in their field be developed. Some interesting common points follow:

> Geographers employed in American colleges and universities for too long have been hired to do one job and rewarded for doing another. (Association of American Geographers, special committee,1994, p. 1)

Most faculty in most institutions find the "research—scholarship paradigm" a noble aspiration, yet peripheral to how they lead their daily professional lives. They are drawn to classroom teaching and time with students, community service, applied projects and consulting. This is particularly true in sociology, which thrives on social activism, social change, and enfranchisement of disadvantaged groups. (Task Force of the American Sociological Association, 1996, p. 7)

For history, the privilege given to the monograph in promotion and tenure has led to the undervaluing of other activities central to the life of the discipline—writing textbooks, developing courses and curricula, documentary editing, museum exhibitions, and film projects to name a few. (American Historical Association, Ad Hoc Committee,1993, p. 1)

After reflecting on its study and findings, the Committee discussed at some length a wide variety of possible recommendations. We came to the conclusion that, given the enormous diversity of institutions of higher education and departments, only one general recommendation can be made:

> "The recognition and rewards system in the mathematical sciences departments must encompass the full array of faculty activity required to fulfill departmental and institutional missions."
>
> We learned from our study of the rewards structure that this perhaps self-evident recommendation is being implemented in only a

small number of departments, and only a somewhat larger number are even beginning to grapple with the issues it entails. There is a clear need for departments to implement the changes that are required to achieve the goal stated in the recommendation. (Joint Policy Board for Mathematics, 1994, p. 27)

While no single definition or conceptualization of scholarship works across disciplines, there is general agreement about the characteristics or features of scholarly, professional, or creative work. Whether it be publishing the results of scholarly research, developing a new course or program, writing an innovative textbook, implementing an outreach program for the community, or directing a student production, faculty on the disciplinary task forces agreed that there are many different activities that exhibit the scholarly, professional, or creative qualities associated with promotion, tenure, and merit recognition. While the relative weight given to any activity is highly context—dependent, six features seem to characterize the work that most disciplines would consider scholarly:

Features of Scholarly and Professional Work
- The activity requires a high level of discipline—related expertise
- The activity breaks new ground, is innovative
- The activity can be replicated or elaborated
- The work and its results can be documented
- The work and its results can be peer—reviewed
- The activity has significance or impact (Diamond and Adam, 1993).

Focusing on these features of scholarly, creative, or intellectual work rather than on a particular conceptualization of scholarship has the advantage of speaking to faculty across the disciplines since it gets away from what the work is called or the site in which the work takes place and focuses attention on the qualities of the work itself. These features or qualities can be used as criteria when considering the full range of faculty work within the scholarly domain, including traditional research and publication.

DIFFERENCES AMONG THE DISCIPLINES

Disciplinary differences emerged as the statements were developed. Important distinctions include the following.

The disciplines understand and define "scholarship" differently. Unique epistemology and disciplinary practices shape the boundaries for scholarly work and must be honored in order for disciplinary values to complement institutional values.

As the chemistry scholars pointed out in their statement (American Chemical Society Task Force, 1993), "it is far less important to worry about what things are called than it is to recognize and nurture important activities." While in chemistry "the words scholarship and research have become nearly synonymous in referring to the discovery of new knowledge," (p. 8) in the Interdisciplinary Task Force for the arts (1993), "the word 'work' is used in the title's text because it provides an umbrella . . . necessary because definitions of such terms as creative activity, research, scholarship, teaching, and service can be narrow or broad" (p. 2). The fact that the disciplines use different language to describe their work and mean different things when they use particular language has ramifications for any cross—disciplinary peer review, such as the present promotion and tenure process on most campuses (Diamond, 1994, p. 10). It is important that language be a point of negotiation in faculty review processes.

Models or paradigms, like language, work differently for the disciplines. While some disciplines in our project (e.g., history and sociology) were comfortable with the four categories of scholarship conceptualized in Ernest Boyer's *Scholarship Reconsidered* (1990) (scholarship of discovery, integration, application, and teaching), other disciplines (e.g., the arts) were not. The American Assembly of Collegiate Schools of Business's statement (Laidlaw, 1993) used a modification of these categories; other disciplines built their statements around the traditional triad of research, teaching, and service (language, geography, chemistry, journalism, and religion). The arts (1994) developed a unique framework appropriate for their disciplines. The Geological Society of America's Task Force began in 1993 with the categories of research, application, and teaching, but, used the traditional triad of teaching, research, and service in the 1996 revision of their document. Although certainly complicating, these multiple definitions and schemata must be honored in the faculty reward system. The degree to which faculty find the present reward system problematic differs both individually and across disciplines. Some disciplines have found the scientific paradigm a good fit, while others have struggled to make this model work for faculty in their field.

The more comfortable faculty are with the present reward system, the greater the possibility that they will resist any fundamental change in the ways in which their work is valued and rewarded. It was clear from the *National Study on the Relative Importance of Research and Undergraduate Teaching at Colleges and Universities* (Gray, Diamond and Adam, 1996) that many faculty, particularly in the sciences, envision their departments losing resources, and consequently power, if the present reward system is modified. For those disciplines that have emphasized research over the last decade in order to improve their positions in the academy, efforts to broaden conceptions of faculty work can seem dangerously regressive. Engaging such faculty in change initiatives is an important challenge.

Certain faculty activities are more central to particular disciplines than to others. This centrality may be related to epistemology or to more practical matters such as continuance of the discipline or the particular needs of students within the field of study.

The Association of American Geographers' statement (1994) argues that "teaching is an especially critical faculty role in geography programs for two reasons. First, the integrative and synthetic nature of geography demands clear and coherent exposition. Second, few students enter colleges and universities intending to major in geography" (p. 7). The sociologists' statement (1994) argues for the importance of student advising to their work as faculty—scholars, noting that their "courses attract a lot of non—traditional and under—prepared students, and (overlapping but not identical) a high population of minority students." The sociology statement continues, "As a profession we are proud of these commitments, but recognize the large number of office hours devoted to quality professional practice as advisers and mentors" (p. 11).

The Modern Language Association's task force (MLA Commission, 1996) focused on the area of service which they described as "an unwieldy, confused category, encompassing almost any faculty work that falls outside research and scholarship or teaching" (p. 10). Their document enumerates a wide range of activities in which faculty engage under the heading of service. As the title of the document suggests, it was the authors' intent to "make visible" important work in the area of professional service and to make a case for such work in the fields of language and literature.

When considering the promotion and tenure process, it is important to keep in mind the myriad activities in which faculty members are expected to engage under the broad categories of teaching and service. If such activities are expected of faculty and, therefore, are a legitimate part of the faculty role, they should be recognized and evaluated. Historically, college faculty have performed work that "counts" and work that "doesn't count." It is important to consider that many activities may have strong merit within the teaching or service dimensions and satisfy the criteria for scholarly, professional, or creative work as well.

APPLYING THE CRITERIA FOR SCHOLARLY, PROFESSIONAL, AND CREATIVE WORK

While certain types of faculty work are more central to one discipline than to another, it is the responsibility of academic departments to identify and describe the primary activities for its faculty members. The department establishes these priorities within the context of the institutional mission and the goals and values of the unit and the academic discipline. It is *not* the role of the institutional or school/college promotion and tenure committee to decide what constitutes scholarship in a particular field. It is, however, their responsibility to determine if the work being reviewed fits within the stated priorities of the unit and institution, if formal policies and procedures have been followed, and if, in the judgment of disciplinary experts, the work under consideration is significant and of high quality.

The truth is that many research projects and refereed publications do not move their fields ahead, do not break new ground, and are neither innovative nor significant. At the same time, there are activities that are central to the life of the discipline, to the interests of the individual faculty member, and to the priorities and mission of the academic unit and the institution that are not being recognized in the faculty reward system. For example, while textbooks have traditionally been shunned as scholarly publications, a particular text might represent a major breakthrough in how a field is introduced to students. Such a text could have national impact and might invite new pedagogies to develop within the field. Directing a student drama production, developing educational software, or initiating a community literacy project are examples of the types of activities that have traditionally been given little recognition in the faculty reward system, and yet these activities may well meet the six criteria for scholarly work presented earlier.

Faculty serving on promotion and tenure committees need to be prepared to recognize a wide range of faculty roles, different but equally important strengths, and important differences among the disciplines. Institutional priorities must, of course, be considered as central to any decisions concerning the faculty who work in a particular context. The authors of the report of the MLA Commission on Professional Service (1996) spoke for all the disciplines when they said:

> We wanted to make quite sure that the diversity of higher education institutions was represented in our final document. But we were also concerned to provide a general framework for comparing institutional practices and for ensuring the transferability of faculty rewards across institutions. Thus we hoped to reach a definition of faculty rewards that would be valid globally, but with the understanding that these rewards would need to be weighted differently at the local level. We have ultimately left judgment up to the individual institutions. (p. 6)

Any faculty review committee must begin by understanding its role and the limitations of that role. It is, concomitantly, the responsibility of faculty candidates to provide review committees with carefully prepared, well-organized documentation of their work.

DOCUMENTATION: THE PROFESSIONAL PORTFOLIO

Some faculty bristle at the word *documentation,* believing that the importance of their work should be self—evident, or that the complexity of their work makes rich representation impossible, or that it is the job of the promotion and tenure committee to "discover" the merits of the their case. We believe that it is the candidate's responsibility to make the case for his or her work and its significance. Mentoring or advising of new faculty should include planning for how the candidate's work will be documented for review.

The portfolio has been used over the past decade to represent the teaching life of a professor. We suggest a more inclusive portfolio that pulls together a professor's teaching, research, and service activities. A carefully selected set of documents, artifacts, testimonials, and data can present a strong case for one's full contribution to the institution. Making the case for one's work can best be done in consultation with a colleague or mentor and takes place over time. The process of learning about what it means to be a professor becomes part of the portfolio, represented in a reflective statement or faculty essay. Like the teaching portfolio as described by Peter Seldin and Associates (1993), the professional portfolio includes multiple perspectives including perceptions by self, colleagues and peers, and students (pp. 6—7). Other perspectives may be appropriate as well. The professional portfolio provides the faculty member being reviewed with the opportunity to describe the range of activities in which he or she has been engaged and to explain the rationale for and significance of those activities. It is then the candidate's responsibility to provide supportive materials that will allow disciplinary colleagues to judge the quality and significance of the work as portrayed in the portfolio.

Portfolio documents and artifacts can be collected from a number of sources (see Figure 4.1). It is important to emphasize that a "selected" portfolio must be focused and manageable, providing a collection of materials that can be reviewed in depth. Since portfolios serve multiple purposes, such as ongoing professional development, it is important to distinguish such practices from the professional portfolio used for assessment purposes. The professional portfolio, as we are describing it, is not prepared annually, although collection of materials may be an ongoing process. This selected set of materials is used at the time of major decisions, such as promotion, tenure, or merit review. Preparing a portfolio for assessment purposes is a time—consuming task; it is not cost—effective to do so on an annual basis.

For the professional portfolio, we suggest that faculty be advised to select three or four accomplishments in the scholarly domain and submit full documentation of these activities including evidence or substantiation of significance and quality. The review committee has the opportunity to review these submissions within the context provided by the faculty candidate. The practice of counting and attributing some arbitrary weight to publications or presentations does not take into account the significance of the work or its relationship to departmental and institutional mission nor does it take into account how and why the candidate chose to conduct the work and what he or she considers its relative merit to be.

THE FACULTY ESSAY

The initial document in the professional portfolio is the faculty essay— a descriptive and reflective piece that provides a frame of reference or a

Figure 4.1 Some examples of sources of documentation

(From R.M. Diamond, 1994. *Serving on Promotion and Tenure Committees: A Faculty Guide.* Bolton, MA: Anker.)

Establishing Quality
- Expert testimony (formal reviews, juries, and solicited testimony)
- Faculty essay (describing the process that was followed, the rationale behind decisions that were made, and the quality of the products)
- Formal reports and studies
- Publication, display, or presentation (video—based or multimedia)

Establishing Significance
- Faculty essay (explaining why the work is important, to whom, and for what purposes)
- External reviews focusing on the significance and usefulness of the activity/product
- Impact on the intended audience
  —Size and scope
  —Documentation (changes in learning, attitudes, performance)
- Relation to the mission statement of the institution/department
- Documentation of individual assignment (What is the department expecting of the faculty member?)
- Disciplinary statement reinforcing type of work involved

---

context for the materials submitted in the portfolio. This central text in the portfolio is designed to create a context for readers, describing what is there and why it has been included. The faculty essay provides important information for consideration in the promotion, tenure, or review process, such as:

- Rationale for choices the faculty member made concerning his or her work, including selections for the portfolio
- An organizational framework for the materials presented
- The faculty member's expectations and the degree to which they were realized
- Circumstances that supported or constrained the candidate's success

- Important issues around the work of the candidate from his or her perspective
- The significance of the work from the candidate's perspective

It is important to bear in mind the distinction between the faculty essay and the work itself. It is the purpose of the portfolio to provide documentation of the faculty member's work and its quality and significance. The descriptive essay enhances reviewers' understanding of the candidate's work but cannot substitute for documentation of the work or evidence of its significance. Providing background and personal reflection and insight creates a strong context for reviewing the portfolio contents. The faculty essay, however, cannot make the candidate's case; the professional portfolio makes the case by portraying the candidate's work through multiple lenses, only one of which is the candidate's own.

ASSESSING FACULTY WORK:
THE EXPERT JUDGMENT OF PEERS

A carefully constructed professional portfolio presents a review committee with good information on which to make judgments, but judgments still must be made and are neither easy nor self-evident. A strong context and solid documentation along with clear policies and guidelines provide the basis for good decision making, but decisions are made by humans who bring a complex set of beliefs, assumptions, and expectations to the assessment along with distinct disciplinary perspectives and personal preferences. Since promotion, tenure, and merit decisions take place within institutional environments that are highly political, an added dimension must be acknowledged about the assessment context. Untangling these complex dynamics is a difficult challenge. Colleagues' best intentions can be thwarted by unacknowledged assumptions, and peers' judgments can be influenced by political posturing of influential committee members. Developing trust in evaluation practices as well as among the colleagues who will make these important judgments is crucial to improving assessment practices. Providing opportunities for review committees to become adept at working together is part of the process of professional development. New members of review teams need to be socialized and oriented in order to perform their roles well. In short, preparing for assessment is a process involving faculty candidates as well as those who will evaluate their work. This important professional development function should be part of a systematic institutional assessment plan.

In Part Two of the Council of Administrators of family and Consumer Sciences' statement (1994), "Documentation of Faculty Work," Jerelyn Schultz states, "The potential Achilles heel of the movement to refocus the priorities of faculty are perceived barriers related to documenting and evaluating faculty work" (p. 10). It is ironic that in an institution that conducts assessment of students on a regular basis, we still have so little faith in assessment practices. Perhaps this has to do with the individualistic manner in which the faculty role has taken shape. While peer review is an accepted practice in the scholarly domain, teaching has remained an individual act. Edgerton, Hutchings, and Quinlan (1991) suggest that since "teaching tends to be a private, solitary activity, collaboratively—designed portfolios are an antidote to this isolation and a way to promote collegial exchange focused on the substance—the scholarship—of teaching" (p. 5).

Most of the literature on faculty assessment assumes a separation of considerations of scholarly contributions from considerations of one's teaching. Separating the domains of faculty work in this way perpetuates a fragmented view of faculty work and reinforces the distinction between the work that counts and the work that doesn't. Envisioning ways to present a full picture of one's work seems useful in integrating the various activities of one's scholarly and professional life. The portfolio provides a process and a mechanism for portraying the full range of a faculty member's work. It also provides an opportunity to reflect on one's work and to fold that reflection into the assessment. Lee Shulman (1988) describes portfolios as

> messy to construct, cumbersome to store, and vulnerable to misrepresentation. But in ways no other assessment method can, portfolios provide a connection to the context and personal histories that characterize real teaching and make it possible to document the unfolding of both teaching and learning over time (p.37).

Providing a strong context and a map of the intersections of one's teaching, service, and research make the professional portfolio a medium for representing the richness of faculty work and for helping colleagues from other disciplines to understand and appreciate that work. Review committees find that a carefully constructed portfolio leads them through a collection of documents and artifacts and provides multiple "looks" at a candidate's work. However, there is no getting around the fact that reviewing a colleague's dossier, portfolio, or CV requires interpretation and judgment. Quality and significance are not self—evident. For this reason, it is important that reviewers appreciate the boundaries around what they know and can judge and what they do and cannot know. Assessments about the quality and significance of a disciplinary scholar's work are best made by peers in the discipline. What reviewers from other disciplines can assess is how well policies and procedures have been followed, how well the candidate's strengths fit within the departmental goals and mission, and how well the department's criteria for promotion or tenure seem to be met by this candidate's work—in other words, process-related and policy-related issues.

SUPPORTING AND GUIDING NEW FACULTY

Most campuses have some provision for mentoring of new faculty, although these arrangements are often informal and inconsistent across or within academic units. It is important that newly appointed faculty members be provided with support and guidance as they prepare for promotion or tenure. Institutional priorities vary as do specific departmental procedures. Faculty candidates need complete information about the review process. They also need access to knowledgeable colleagues and published material related to faculty review practices. There is a growing body of literature that can assist faculty preparing for promotion or tenure review. In *Preparing for Promotion and Tenure Review* (Diamond, 1995), faculty will find guidelines for portfolio development, examples of documentation strategies for non-traditional scholarly work, and a checklist of things to do and consider as they prepare for review. (The checklist is outlined in Figure 4.2).

One area in which faculty need support and guidance is the evaluation of their teaching. Historically, student course ratings have served as the central measure of faculty effectiveness. Student evaluations are only one of an array of instruments and strategies that can be employed to assess teaching and student learning. Academic departments need to explore the range of available options and assist faculty in choosing ones appropriate for their discipline, teaching style, and pedagogy. Figure 4.3 suggests one plan for evaluating teaching. It is important that departments take the time to educate both the faculty candidate and the promotion and tenure committee about alternative methods for representing and evaluating teaching effectiveness.

Figure 4.2 Preparing for promotion and tenure: A faculty check list
(From, Robert M. Diamond, 1995. *Preparing for Promotion and Tenure Review: A Faculty Guide,* Bolton, MA: Anker.)

Basic Requirements
☐ Have you included all the items required by your department and school/college guidelines?

Cover Letter or Faculty Essay
Does your cover letter or faculty essay provide guidelines that will help the committee review your materials? Have you discussed
☐ The significance of your work from your perspective?
☐ The major challenges you faced and what you accomplished?
☐ The major decisions you made and why you made them?
☐ The circumstances that promoted or inhibited success?
☐ The rationale for the materials you have included in your documentation?
☐ The relationship of your work to the priorities of your department, school/college, institution, and discipline?

Teaching
In documenting the quality of your teaching, have you
☐ Presented evidence of planning and course design (organization)?
☐ Presented evidence of student learning?
☐ Included student ratings showing comparison with other faculty?
☐ Included student ratings showing evidence of improvement (where appropriate)?
☐ Showed evidence of effectively appropriate instructional techniques?
☐ Showed evidence of positive impact on retention?

Scholarly/Professional/Creative Work
☐ If you have conducted research and/or published, have you documented the quality and the significance of this work?
☐ Have you included statements from qualified external reviewers?
☐ If appropriate, have you included videos of performance or related activities or included other appropriate visual materials?
☐ If you have developed innovative instructional materials or written a textbook, have you included external reviews or student performance data that address both the significance and the quality of your work?

(continued next page)

Advising
☐ Have you documented the quality of your advising?

Community Service
☐ Have you documented service, outreach, or citizenship
   (department, school/college, institution, community)?

General
☐ Have you eliminated all redundant material?
☐ Have you prepared your material in a way that will communicate
   effectively with colleagues from other disciplines?
☐ Have you included a table of contents to assist the committee in
   locating specific items?
☐ Have you had someone else review your materials?

Figure 4.3 Planning for evaluating teaching

(From J. Centra, R. Froh, P. Gray, L. Lambert, and R. Diamond, 1987. *A Guide
to Evaluating Teaching for Promotion and Tenure.* Acton, MA: Copley)

Which Characteristics will be Evaluated?
• Good organization of subject matter and course
• Effective communication
• Knowledge of and enthusiasm for the subject matter and teaching
• Positive attitudes toward students
• Fairness in assessment and grading
• Flexibility in approaches to teaching
• Appropriate student learning outcomes

How will Data be Collected?
• Self-assessment/report
• Classroom observation
• Structured interview
• Instructional rating survey
• Test or appraisal of student achievement
• Content analysis of instructional materials
• Review of classroom records

Who will do the Evaluating?
• Self   • Dean or department chair
• Students   • Alumni
• Faculty   • Other appropriate administrators

ASSESSMENT: A CONTEXT-SPECIFIC ACTIVITY

In reviewing each faculty candidate's "case," the review committee must be confident that they know of any agreements or expectations that were established at the time the candidate was recruited and hired. If there are no formal documents substantiating such agreements, the candidate and the department chair should be consulted and their understandings considered equally. Existing policy statements, guidelines, and other pertinent documents should be consulted so that the committee understands the criteria and terms under which the candidate was working. It is not the place of the promotion and tenure committee to challenge or question such policies or documents, assuming they were approved through proper institutional channels. Since such guidelines and policy statements change over time, it is important that the policies in effect at the time of the candidate's appointment be considered for tenure and that the application of criteria for promotion be guided by departmental or college policy statements. How well the candidate's work fits with the institutional and departmentals missions is certainly an applicable criterion for the review committee to apply.

Essentially, it is important that each candidate's work be "considered situationally within the department and institution and with respect to the academic discipline and the strengths and interests of the individual" (Diamond, 1994, p. 9). A checklist for promotion and tenure committees is outlined in Figure 4.4. Developing such a checklist for a particular institutional context is a useful activity for those involved in promotion and tenure review. In the process of identifying the steps in the process and naming the various aspects to be considered, reviewers are challenged to articulate their assumptions and expectations and are reminded of the complexity of their task.

Our contention is that the context is the all—important variable in assessing faculty work. What constitutes a strong, significant contribution depends upon the demands of the individual situation. Those within the context need to have the authority to shape the criteria that will be used therein. The values of the history department need not be the values of the engineering school. Nor should the criteria applied to a faculty candidate's portfolio in a research university be the same as those applied in a liberal arts college setting. The single set of criteria, or one-size-fits-all model, cannot work across contexts. Those who advocate a single set of assessment criteria across departmental, school/college, or institutional contexts argue that fairness requires that the same values and expectations be brought to bear in all cases. This approach dismisses the fundamental differences that mark disciplinary and institutional contexts. fairness is not sameness. Rather, fair assessment of individuals in different contexts requires a separate-but-equal approach that seeks to identify those values or features that can be viewed across contexts and to isolate the aspects that are most salient in the particular context. The generic approach employed by many institutions discourages faculty from venturing into new territory, from taking risks, from pursuing ideas or activities that do not fit the one-size model. Students and society deserve the best that faculty have to offer, and reward systems should support faculty inquiry, innovation, and invention. Situating the assessment process within a specific context honors the importance of institutional priorities and the unique contributions made by individual faculty.

Figure 4.4 Promotion and tenure committee checklist

(From Robert M. Diamond, 1994. *Serving on Promotion and Tenure Committees: A Faculty Guide.* Bolton, MA: Anker.

Basic Information
- ☐ Review institutional, school/college, and departmental guidelines and polices for promotion and tenure
- ☐ Review disciplinary/departmental statements describing the scholarly/professional work of faculty
- ☐ Review specific assignments of candidate and supporting documentation
- ☐ Review procedures for documenting and evaluating the professional work of faculty, including teaching, advising, and service

Information to Candidate
- ☐ The type of documentation the committee expects
- ☐ The specific steps that will be followed
- ☐ The criteria that will be used to assess the quality of materials provided

The Review Process
Teaching
- ☐ Good organization of subject matter and course
- ☐ Effective communication

☐ Knowledge of and enthusiasm for the subject matter and teaching
☐ Positive attitude toward students
☐ Fairness in assessment and grading
☐ Flexibility in approaches to teaching
☐ Appropriate student learning outcomes

Advising
☐ Accessibility
☐ Quality of interchange
☐ Knowledge

Service, Nondisciplinary (Citizenship)
☐ Range and significance of activities
☐ Quality of participation

Scholarly/Professional Work
☐ Attains high level of discipline-related expertise
☐ Breaks new ground, is innovative
☐ Can be replicated or elaborated
☐ Can be documented
☐ Can be peer-reviewed

REWARDING FACULTY WORK

As we approach the twenty-first century, American higher education faces many challenges. The various publics we serve are asking legitimate questions about faculty roles, and faculty are asking equally legitimate questions about the rewards for their work. The American higher education system is the envy of the world because it has enlarged its collective mission to reach out to many students and to serve many community and societal needs. The faculty reward system needs to reflect the inclusive spirit of American higher education, and honor and reward the many facets of faculty work. A system that accommodates the complex interplay of institutional, disciplinary, and individual differences will best serve the needs of colleges and universities, academic departments, disciplines, and individual teacher—scholars. Ultimately, all involved in the higher education enterprise will share the benefit of more complete understandings about the faculty role, better documentation of the various aspects of that role, and a faculty reward system that is sensitive to the strengths of individuals, the contexts in which they work, and the unique characteristics of the academic disciplines.

REFERENCES

American Chemical Society Task Force on the Definition of Scholarship in Chemistry. (1993). *Report of the American Chemical Society Task Force on the Definition of Scholarship in Chemistry.* Washington, DC: American Chemical Society.

American Historical Association Ad Hoc Committee on Redefining Scholarly Work. (1993). *Redefining Historical Scholarship.* Washington, DC: American Historical Association.

Association of American Geographers Special Committee on Faculty Roles and Rewards. (1994). *Reconsidering faculty roles and rewards.* Washington, DC: Association of American Geographers.

Boyer, E. (1990). *Scholarship reconsidered.* Princeton, NJ: Carnegie Foundation for the Advancement of Teaching.

Centra, J., Froh, R., Gray, P., Lambert, L., and Diamond, R. (1987). *A guide to evaluating teaching for promotion and tenure.* Acton, MA: Copley.

Council of Administrators of Family and Consumer Sciences. (1994). *Recognition and rewards in the family and consumer sciences.* Northridge, CA.

Diamond, R. (1994). *Serving on promotion and tenure review: A faculty guide.* Bolton, MA: Anker.

———. (1995). *Preparing for promotion and tenure review: A faculty guide.* Bolton, MA: Anker.

Diamond, R. and Adam, B. (1993). Recognizing faculty work: Reward systems for the year 2000. *New Directions for Higher Education, 81,* 13—22.

———. (1995). *The disciplines speak: Rewarding the scholarly, professional, and creative work of faculty.* Washington, DC: American Association for Higher Education.

Edgerton, R., Hutchings, P., & Quinlan, K. (1991). *The teaching portfolio: Capturing the scholarship in teaching.* Washington, DC: American Association for Higher Education.

Geological Society of America Task Force on the Definition of Scholarship in the Geosciences. (1996). *Scholarship in the geosciences.* Boulder, CO: the Geological Society of America.

Gray, P., Diamond, R., and Adam, B. (1966). *A national study on the relative importance of research and undergraduate teaching at colleges and universities.* Syracuse, NY: Syracuse University.

Interdisciplinary Task Force. (1994). *The work of arts faculties in higher education.* Reston, VA: National Office for Arts Accreditation in Higher Education.

Joint Policy Board for Mathematics Committee on Professional Recognition and Rewards. (1994). *Recognition and rewards in the mathematical sciences.* Washington, DC: American Mathematical Society

Laidlaw, W. (1993). *Defining scholarly work in management education.* St. Louis, MO: American Assembly of Collegiate Schools of Business.

Modern Language Association Commission on Professional Service. (1996, December). *Making faculty work visible: Reinterpreting professional service, teaching, and research in the fields of language and literature.* New York, Modern Language Association of America.

Seldin, P. and Associates. (1993). *Successful use of teaching portfolios.* Bolton, MA: Anker

Shulman, L. (1988). A union of insufficiencies: Strategies for teacher assessment in a period of educational reform. *Educational Leadership,* 46(3), 36–41.

A Task Force of the American Sociological Association. (1996). *Recognizing and rewarding the professional and scholarly work of sociologists.* Washington, DC: American Sociological Association.

Wiedman, L. and Cummings, M. (1993). *Report of the Geological Society of America Task Force on the Definition of Scholarship in the Geosciences.* Boulder, CO: Geological Society of America.

CHAPTER 5

Faculty Salary Structures in Research Universities
Implications for Productivity

James C. Hearn
University of Minnesota

Faculty salaries are a prominent feature of the reward systems under which academic work is done. Not surprisingly, therefore, they are also becoming a rather prominent element in the recent attention to college and university productivity. Among those examining salaries in recent years have been legislators curious over how $100,000 a year professors spend their time, journalists worried about rises in tuition rates, attorneys investigating charges of discrimination in hiring and promotions, and faculty concerned about salary imbalances within and across academic departments. Also increasingly interested in salary structures have been central administrators looking for ways to manage rising costs. Because faculty salaries are usually the largest single item in academic budgets, they are unquestionably central to the productivity of the enterprise.

The growing internal and external attention to salaries has brought to light the need to develop both conceptualizations and policies in this arena. Too much of the recent attention to the topic has been based on anecdotal and incomplete information.[1] This paper is aimed at providing those interested in salaries with a more expansive and more balanced perspective. The major focus here is on research universities, the setting in which many of the current controversies over salaries have arisen.

The chapter first investigates the historical roots of faculty salary structures. Next, it examines salaries as an element in university reward systems, the tenuous relationship between salaries and performance on campus, policy choices for those developing university salary systems, and criteria for judging institutional salary systems. The chapter closes with some thoughts on the significance of salaries for leaders seeking more effective academic reward systems.[2] The ultimate goal of the essay is to help leaders craft salary policies that improve productivity in their institutions.

THE HISTORICAL ROOTS OF FACULTY SALARY STRUCTURES

In the earliest years of this country, colleges were often hard-nosed in their efforts to limit faculty pay. According to Rudolph (1990), the financially stressed colleges of the nineteenth century asked, in effect, that faculty become "philanthropists" by accepting lowered salaries or by allowing salary payments to be delayed. To help such practices endure, many political, civic, and educational leaders publicly lauded the estimable qualities of the providers and receivers of poor pay. For example, President Charles Eliot in his inaugural address at Harvard in 1869 (Rudolph, 1990) mused that the low pay of faculty was actually a national virtue

> The poverty of scholars is of inestimable worth in this money-getting nation. It maintains the true standards of virtue and honor. The poor scholars and preachers of duty defend the modern community against its own material prosperity. Luxury and learning are ill bed-fellows. (p. 196)

In a similar vein, politicians of the era consistently echoed the view of the Iowa legislators who argued in an 1847 report that "those who labor in the work of education, to be successful, must be endowed with such love of their profession as will make them content with less remuneration than can be obtained in ordinary business" (p.196). The words of Cardinal Newman well represented views among public and educational leaders as well as faculty in that era: "Such is the constitution of the human mind, that any kind of knowledge, if it really be such, is its own reward" (p. 78).

Some professors of the time, albeit with little choice otherwise, obligingly accepted their low salaries as a form of noble sacrifice (p.196). Unquestionably, however, the material incentives for working well were weak. In the words of Brown president Francis Wayland in 1842, the poor pay of faculty "removed all the ordinary stimulants to professional effort" (p.200). As Rudolph wryly notes of the period, "There are all kinds of psychic incomes, but it is doubtful whether many college professors thought that salving the conscience of a materialistic society was really a justification for their inadequate salaries" (p.196).

Institutional parsimony, accompanied by loftily phrased expectations for faculty complicity in that parsimony, continued well into the twentieth century.[3] Harvard's President Eliot reiterated in 1908 his views of earlier years: "The profession can never be properly recruited by holding out pecuniary inducements"(p.196).[4]

For a brief period in the 1920s and early 1930s, faculty salaries did rise relative to those in other occupations. The ratio of average faculty salaries to average earnings in industry reached a new high of 3.6 in 1932 (Freeman, 1979). Journalists and external observers on the left and right seemed to prefer the traditional deficit in pay, however. In 1930 the *Nation* magazine noted, "Boost the professors as a group into the high salaried class . . . and you create a strongly entrenched university vested interest in the status quo. Rich professors are all too often social Bourbons" (Rudolph, 1990, p. 197). In a similar vein, the *New Republic* noted in 1929 that low salaries freed professors from "the pecuniary criterion of value," and were therefore to be praised (ibid.). By the late 1930s, the ratio of faculty to industrial salaries had fallen to levels around 2.5 (Freeman, 1979).

The ratio remained rather constant at that level after the Depression years. A specific comparison with salaries among other professionals confirms the conclusion that faculty salaries ran at a deficit from the Depression years into the 1970s. While physicians and attorneys received large salaries in return for sacrificing financially during their years of post-baccalaureate education, the financial returns to comparable years of education toward a Ph.D. remained rather low, and especially so for those who chose to remain in academic settings (Tuckman, 1976; Dillon and Marsh, 1981).

Historical Patterns in Salaries in Research Universities.

Clearly, one of the biggest structural changes in higher education in this century has been the emergence and growth of the research university sector. Perhaps surprisingly, this development in the early and middle decades of the century did not radically alter the general patterns in faculty pay. Although university faculty (and especially faculty in professional schools such as law and medicine) began to earn more than faculty in other institutions, faculty in most fields in most universities faced from the beginning base salary rates relatively low in relation to those in other professionalized fields (Caplow and McGee, 1958).

The research university for many years resembled other institutions in the relative invisibility of salary issues. As late as the 1960s, Brown (1965) found the determination of faculty salaries at these and other institutions to be "carefully clothed in secrecy" (p.154).[5] A decade later, other social scientists (see Katz, 1973; Freeman, 1975) found the subject of university faculty's salaries still little examined. Analysts attributed this lack of attention to the absence of useful national data and to the reluctance of institutions to reveal their faculty evaluation and reward processes (ibid.). The emerging centrality of the academic department as the primary sanctioning unit for faculty in research universities may also have thwarted attempts at institution-wide or across-institution salary analyses. As research-oriented institutions began to develop, faculty in different disciplines communicated with each other less frequently than in earlier institutions and earlier years, and top administrators began to defer to unit heads the responsibility of setting individual salaries (Clark, 1983). This decentralization of salary control, and to an extent salary data, may have helped discourage analysis and dialogue concerning salary patterns (Hansen, 1988b).

Whether for organizational barriers, lack of data, traditional allegiances to the larger rewards of academic life, or some other reason, most research university faculty prior to the current era did not complain very loudly or mobilize collectively regarding their salaries. Even in the context of declines in the 1970s in real and comparative faculty pay, (see Clotfelter, 1996) salaries tended not to be a prominent issue on research university campuses. Faculty labor unions were formed on many other campuses in the 1960s, 1970s, and 1980s, but only rarely were they successfully organized at research universities, and university faculties' attitudes toward unionization on their campuses often depended more on working conditions and job security than on financial concerns (see Lawler and Walker, 1980; Becker, 1985).[6]

In sum, prior to the 1990s, research universities reflected a distinctive normative legacy concerning faculty salaries. Simply put, that legacy suggested to all concerned that the main rewards of academic life lay beyond mere finances and that, relatedly, faculty salaries were not problematic enough to merit extended policy debate or aggressive mobilization. Burton Clark (1987) translated this normative legacy into a syllogism which, he argued, represents "the sustaining myth" of academic careers in this country: education is critical to the hopes of humanity and, therefore, the limited material rewards provided by a faculty career are overshadowed by the richness of other kinds of rewards (p.222).[7] Clark cited national survey data supporting his view of faculty's attitudes towards the financial and nonfinancial rewards of their careers. Further support for his inferences comes from a finding that a majority of U.S. research university faculty in the late 1980s labeled themselves "satisfied" or "very satisfied" with their salaries (U.S. Department of Education, 1990).

Whatever one's views regarding the historical authenticity of Clark's sustaining myth, there are some signs that it could be losing some of its hold on faculty and others in the 1990s. Policymakers have begun to question traditional approaches to tenure and traditional assumptions about the performance of faculty (Tierney and Bensimon, 1996). While tenured faculty have certainly viewed security and autonomy as valued components of their jobs offsetting any deficits in their compensation (Tierney, 1997b), their comfort with existing salary levels and salary policies may decline to the extent their job security is threatened and their working environment becomes less attractive. For those faculty with nonacademic employment opportunities, significant improvement in salaries may be necessary to offset other emerging problems on campus. Yet dramatic salary gains may be unlikely. It can give faculty no comfort that their salaries are the largest single item on university budgets in a time of growing public scrutiny of those budgets. Accountability and productivity pressures from university boards, legislators, and others are raising the visibility of salary issues in the 1990s. A variety of observers and analysts have begun to explore alternatives to the ways salaries are currently rewarded (see e.g., Moore and Amey, 1993; "Poison Ivy?" 1996; Fairweather, 1996; Lewis, 1996). The legacy of secrecy, diffidence, and silence may be giving way.

FACULTY SALARIES IN RESEARCH UNIVERSITIES: WHAT CONTEMPORARY DATA SHOW

The 1940 Statement of Principles of the American Association of University Professors (AAUP) noted that tenure is a means not only to academic freedom but also to "a sufficient degree of economic security to make the profession attractive to men and women of ability (AAUP, 1996a). In other words, academic careers on the traditional tenure track should provide sufficient financial rewards to maintain commitment and loyalty. Recent data on the success of research institutions in meeting that goal in the 1990s are mixed.

Salaries Relative to Inflation

In the 1990s, the salaries of university faculty are no longer regularly losing ground relative to inflation, as indexed by the consumer price index (CPI). When adjusted for inflation using the CPI, average salaries seem to have bottomed out in the early 1980s. Since that time, they have rebounded to a level roughly equal to that of the early 1970s (Clotfelter, 1996; AAUP, 1997). In the most recent data available (1996–97), salary gains roughly paralleled inflation (AAUP, 1997). Recent concerns that the CPI overstates inflation have led some to suggest examining salary trends over time using a reduced inflation index. When examined using the CPI minus one point, faculty salaries may actually be as much as 15 percent above their levels in 1972–73 (AAUP, 1996b). Of course, overall data of this kind do not illuminate salary variations among individuals, fields, and institutions. Still, it must be concluded that the aggregate data give no sign of a crisis in faculty salaries: the past quarter-century has brought neither dramatically falling nor dramatically rising faculty salaries in research universities.

Salaries Relative to Total Income

Faculty's base nine-month academic salaries are not their only sources of potential income. Bowen and Schuster (1986) suggest faculty earnings fall into four categories: base contract pay for 9 months, extra contract pay for 11 or 12 months, extra pay ad hoc for special services such as summer work or overloads during the academic year, and earnings from sources outside the institution for consulting and other services (see also Boyer and Lewis, 1984). Faculty's additional earnings beyond base contract pay are perhaps lower overall than some might suppose, however. Notably, among full-time university faculty who have at least some involvement with undergraduate teaching, well under one-half report spending any time at all on consulting or freelance work, and fewer than one-tenth spend more than four hours a week on such activities (Sax, Astin, Arredondo, and Korn 1996).

Salaries Relative to Other Professional Fields

In the last two decades, long-standing salary differences between academics and other professionals have grown wider. Compared to an index of salaries in professionalized fields outside higher education (health professions, law, engineering, and nonacademic scientists), faculty salaries have lost substantial ground since the late 1970s (AAUP, 1997). Of course, many faculty may find their supplemental earnings and the nonmonetary returns of their careers sufficient to offset any deficit in comparative base pay. When analyses of faculty's individual returns to education focus on base salaries alone, the full range of rewards for faculty careers may be substantially underestimated. Still, the deficit in salaries led Linda Bell, lead analyst for the 1997 AAUP report on salaries, to comment that "the large bulk of us do not earn what some of the most poorly paid professionals [in other fields] earn" (Magner, 1997).

Differences by Institutional Control

Public and private universities differ in average faculty salaries. Inevitably, some of these differences are due to distinctive patterns of program offerings: lower-paying, public service–oriented fields are more frequently represented on public campuses and tend to be proportionately larger in size there, for example. Still, three patterns in public-private salary differences are noteworthy. First, salaries are appreciably higher in each faculty rank in the private institutions (see AAUP, 1997).[8] Notably, full professors in public doctoral institutions in 1996–97 earned on average $72,220, while full professors in private doctoral institutions earned on average $92,112 (AAUP, 1997; see also U.S. Department of Education, 1996). Second, the growth of average faculty salaries in the years since the mid-1980s has been faster overall in private institutions. Specifically, salaries grew 66 percent in the private doctoral sector between 1985–86 and 1995–96, while increasing only 52 percent in the public doctoral sector (AAUP, 1996b). Third, the dispersion of yearly salary gains appears to be appreciably larger in the public sector: individual public institutions are more likely than individual private institutions to award large salary increases in a given year, despite the fact that increases in public institutions overall tend to be smaller on average (see AAUP, 1997).[9] This pattern may be due to the cyclical nature of state economies and appropriations: years of low or no increases may be followed by a year of makeup raises.

Field Differences

In any investigation of salary structures, it is critical to examine data disaggregated by field.[10] Three patterns stand out in recent data. First, salary differences by field are substantial. Full professors of engineering earned on average about $20,000 more than full professors in education at fouryear institutions in 1994–95.[11] Differences between law or medicine faculty and faculty in the liberal arts are even more striking (Hamermesh, 1988). Second, inequality in salaries among fields seems to have grown since the earlier decades of the century (ibid.). Third, and relatedly, some fields have clearly outpaced others in recent salary growth. Tarrant's analysis (1996) of public universities' salary structures over the period 1985–86 to 1995–96 suggests that management faculty's salaries showed a gain of over 2 percent a year beyond inflation, while salaries among faculty in foreign languages and literatures barely managed to keep pace with inflation over those years. Other fields in Tarrant's sample fell between those two extremes.

Gender Differences

Female faculty in higher education earn appreciably less than male faculty, regardless of age or the number of hours worked, and there is no indication of any substantive trend since the late 1970s in the relationship of female to male earnings (AAUP, 1996b).[12] The proportion of female faculty has increased overall, and the new entrants have tended to be in the junior ranks, but that lack of seniority does not seem to play a primary role in women's continuing deficit in earnings. The deficit is primarily associated, instead, with the fact that women are disproportionately located in lower-paying fields without substantial demand outside universities (AAUP, 1997). The relatively few female faculty in business, computer science, and engineering departments tend to be paid far more generously than those in such fields as social work and languages.[13] Nevertheless, within ranks in given fields, there is evidence of gender differences not explainable by other factors (Bellas, 1997).

Racial/Ethnic Differences

There is a striking lack of evidence concerning the relative earnings of different racial/ethnic groups in higher education. Federal attention to affirmative action, along with the independent commitments made by many institutions to increase minority representation on their faculties, have undoubtedly increased the demand for minority scholars, and perhaps put upward pressures on their salaries as well. On the other hand, the number of minority faculty members remains shockingly small (U.S. Department of Education, 1996), and the most reliable recent evidence suggests they may still be at some salary disadvantage: minority faculty salaries in research universities in 1988 averaged over $1,000 less than the average for nonminorities (Fairweather, 1996, p. 229). Minority faculty may tend to be more junior overall than other faculty, and may tend to be in lower-paying fields as well, and those differences might account for some of the salary deficit. [14] Until more targeted analysis is available, however, it is impossible to draw firm conclusions about relative salaries for similarly situated minorities and nonminorities. For now, one can conclude only that marginally improved relative salaries alone are unlikely to end the undersupply of minority faculty (Beaumont, 1985).[15]

Salary Compression

A significant challenge for academic reward systems is salary compression: the shrinking of interrank salary distances due to market conditions. A typical example of compression is the hiring of a junior professor at a salary equal to or above that of a veteran full professor in the same department. In the 1980s, salary compression became a significant problem in management, engineering, and some other fields with labor shortages (Scott and Bereman, 1992; Snyder, McLaughlin, and Montgomery, 1992). Overall, the ratio of assistant and associate professors' salaries to full professors' salaries in doctoral institutions remained remarkably steady over the years 1980–81 to 1995–96 (AAUP, 1997). That is, there was no notable overall change in the historic relationships between salaries at various ranks over that period. By field, however, clear trends do emerge. For example, Tarrant (1996) found that salary compression declined somewhat in engineering but increased in English over the 1985–86 to 1995–96 period.

Intersections of Salary Structures with Seniority Distributions

Faculty in different fields face different seniority structures. In general, a more senior faculty implies higher average salaries and therefore more costs to the institution. Fields with the highest proportions of senior faculty include physics, geology, chemistry, and history; in each, around one-half of all faculty were at the full professor rank in 1994–95 (College and University Personnel Association, 1995). Fields with the most junior faculty composition were nursing, occupational therapy, physical therapy, and library science; in each, the proportion of faculty at the full professor level was under one-sixth (ibid.). Although these distributions can facilitate predictions of future salary distributions in specific fields, changing labor markets and other confounding factors make extended forecasts questionable.

One extended forecast may be made with some confidence, however: the nation's faculty workforce will grow somewhat younger on average over the next two decades and average salary outlays per faculty member after inflation are likely to decline over that period. Faculty hired in the 1960s and 1970s will be retiring in increasing numbers in the coming decade (Hearn and Anderson, 1998). Whether they'll be replaced mainly by faculty in traditional full-time tenure-track appointments is unknown, but their parting from the scene will bring changes in the nature of faculty salary distributions. As Hansen (1985) noted, the shape of the age-salary profile in a unit, an institution, or a system is an important factor in budgeting and planning. Just as the aging of the faculty workforce brought higher salaries and higher budgets in the 1980s, the reverse of that trend in the early years of the twenty-first century may bring some financial savings to institutions, not only through replacement hires at the junior level and canceling of lines in certain units, but also through the hiring of part-time, clinical, and non-tenure-track faculty not receiving full salaries and benefit packages.

Forecasts of aggregated average salaries are not particularly helpful for understanding the futures of salaries at the level of individual faculty within particular ranks and fields. There, real salaries might grow as the demand for faculty workers to replace retirees grows, (see Bowen and Sosa, 1989) or salaries might shrink as trustees, public officials, and taxpayers extol parsimony in concert with improved accountability and productivity.

Intersections of Salary Structures with Faculty Career Stages and Perceived Well-being

It is intriguing to examine salaries in the context of other factors in the professional and personal lives of university faculty. The annual survey of college faculty by the Higher Education Research Institute (HERI) at

UCLA provides some provocative findings on the connections between faculty members' ages and their perceived sources of stress (see Sax et al., 1996).[16] Personal finances were listed as being somewhat or extensively stressful by 75 percent of the faculty under 35 years old, 67 percent of those 35 to 44 years old, 59 percent of those 45 to 54 years old, 46 percent of those 55 to 64, and 36 percent of those over 65. This pattern of declining financial stress by age may be typical for other professions, but it is noteworthy in higher education for at least two reasons. First, Andrew Carnegie's earlier noted worries over the financial well-being of retired college faculty seem, at least on the surface, to have been reasonably addressed. Older faculty approaching retirement are little concerned over finances. Second, younger faculty apparently perceive their financial status as tenuous. It is unclear whether marginally improved salaries alone would significantly ameliorate this perception. The stress may well stem more from the unknowns of the struggle for tenure and promotion than from the inadequacies of current salaries. Still, there is little question that financial matters, whether writ large (long-term financial prospects) or small (current salaries and assets), are very salient in the personal lives of young faculty.

What Determines Salaries?

Many analysts have used sophisticated statistical models to ascertain the factors influencing individual salaries in various kinds of institutions and various fields. Focusing on research universities, for example, Fairweather (1996) found in a 1988 national faculty sample that the critical nonbehavioral factors affecting salaries were rank, being in a private institution, being male, and being in a high-paying field. Each positively influenced salary levels. Fairweather also found several behavioral factors to be influential, including classroom hours, teaching only graduate students, and publications output. These findings generally match those of earlier studies in research universities (see Smart, 1991, and the excellent literature review by Fox, 1985).

Early observers of faculty salaries noted that there is no single academic marketplace, even within a single institutional sector or a single university. Instead, the marketplace is balkanized, largely on the basis of academic disciplines (Caplow and McGee, 1958; Brown, 1965). With this in mind, analysts have addressed the distinctiveness of salary-reward systems by field. Smart and McLaughlin (1978) found that fields varied so substantially in the factors critical to their individual faculty's salaries that attempts to identify singular "institutional reward structures" were seriously misguided. Those authors suggest institutional salary analyses are best done by separating academic units into groups with similar reward systems.[17] Fairweather (1996) recently provided empirical support for that approach: he found that publications tended consistently to play a larger role in salaries in the health sciences and business fields than in the humanities.[18]

What Do Salaries Determine?

Salaries are a major budget item, so they certainly are determinative of the financial status of research institutions, but there is no evidence that salaries strongly affect the attitudes and performance of faculty at those institutions. McKeachie concluded his 1979 review of the research literature on the topic with the observation that, for most faculty, "the level of salary per se is of little motivational consequence" (p.18). No substantial disagreement with this view has arisen since that time. Beyond a certain minimal standard, salaries seem to be secondary elements in the professional lives of faculty. Rank, tenure, recognition by peers, publications, working conditions, and the like are apparently far more important.

Yet salaries are not trivial to faculty. For one thing, salaries may be important simply because they are so apparent to the individual. Adjustments in salary are as regular a feature of academic life as the arrival of wide-eyed new students each fall and the solemnities of the annual commencement exercise. Unlike tenure or promotions, salary changes are an annual event. Indeed, salaries themselves are even more salient: dealing with a paycheck is a monthly or bi-weekly event.

More important, salary gains are emphasized on a symbolic level by faculty as legitimation and recognition of their worth to their home institution (Clark, 1983; Tuckman, 1976). In that vein, *relative* salary and raises can appreciably affect a faculty member's attitudes and performance. As McKeachie (1979) noted, "One interprets one's salary raise in relation to past raises and in relation to the salaries and raises of one's peers (p.18). The importance of relative pay is heightened by its endurance: salary differences tend to persist because salary adjustments in the U.S. university tend to be incremental in nature. In a world of rather small yearly percentage gains, the starting point is critical to the compounding. Therefore, if no major adjustments are made over time, once one is a somewhat underpaid full professor, one is likely to remain a somewhat underpaid full professor, regardless of performance. Indeed, the deficits in dollar terms relative to comparable but better paid colleagues can grow larger while annual percentage gains proceed identically.[19] If information about such patterns is known, and if McKeachie is correct about the motivational importance of relative standing, widening salary disadvantages could bring growing dissatisfaction among affected faculty.

The evidence on the importance of salaries to faculty and to institutions clearly merits more consideration. The heart of the question, both conceptually and from a policy perspective, is the connection between salaries and productivity. Do salaries reflect performance? Does performance affect salaries? How? In the following section, these questions are explored in more detail.

SALARY STRUCTURES AND FACULTY PERFORMANCE: A TENUOUS RELATIONSHIP

In a number of ways, the salary structures of research universities confound the core tenets of both normative equity theory and neoclassical labor market theory. Here, we explore some of these contradictions. First, however, we briefly introduce the two theories, with special attention to their connections to performance and productivity issues.[20]

Equity theory is a value-based, prescriptive perspective. In its most familiar form, it is descended from the classic Aristotelian view that equity in organizations or social groups is achieved through proportionality, or at least ordinal consistency (see Young, 1994). This view translates, in part, into the tenet that organizations should pursue both horizontal and vertical equity in the ways they treat their employees. *Horizontal equity* is exhibited by rewarding those of equal worth to an organization equally. *Vertical equity* is exhibited by rewarding people of greater worth to an organization more generously than those of less worth to the organization. In both domains of equity, worth to the organization is the sole criterion for rewards. Factors irrelevant to organizational performance should be irrelevant to organizational rewards. Unquestionably, salaries are an organizational reward susceptible to equity analysis.

In contrast to equity theory, neoclassical labor market theory is descriptive rather than prescriptive. In its usual form, it suggests that in competitive environments, salaries will be tightly connected to the marginal productivity of labor. That is, workers will be paid an amount approximating their contribution to the firm's output: the stronger the worker's performance, the more he or she is to be rewarded financially (see Freeman, 1979; Beaumont, 1985). If a worker is underpaid, he or she will move to another competitive organization where his or her going worth will be better recognized. The most traditional versions of neoclassical labor market theory would add that those performing a particular set of tasks within an organization (e.g., in a university, teaching, researching, and performing service) would face a rather homogeneous external labor market determining the going price of their labor (i.e., salaries). Less traditional versions of the theory would recognize more variation in external and internal labor markets.

Common to both equity theory and neoclassical labor market theory is the notion that salary and performance in an organization should be tightly connected. No one would suggest that these theories' idealtype notions of the salary-performance relationship would fit any one actual organization, much less any set of actual organizations, and few would agree with every one of the theories' implications for university policy. Still, the theories do have philosophical appeal and do seem to be violated in higher education's salary structures. Exploring those violations may contribute to productive dialogue and policy development. At least seven areas of disjunction in salaries and performance deserve our attention. Several of these have been introduced earlier, but they are discussed here in more detail.

Organizational Ambiguities in the Enterprise:

There are a number of ways academic organizations, and especially research universities, differ from the profit-seeking firms depicted in classical labor market theories. For one, organizational goals tend to be contested, multiple, and ambiguous. Units in the organization may dissent on what the institution is all about, and these disagreements are resolved through the acceptance of diverse, often vaguely phrased goals. The differences surrounding goals can also extend to the individual level. To a greater extent than classical theories would predict, faculty may be motivated by nonpecuniary factors (such as disciplinary ambition) only loosely connected to the interests of their home institutions (Marsh and Stafford, 1967). Relatedly, the technology for achieving goals tends to be unclear in universities. Modes of instruction are extremely varied, and admissions standards, grading standards, curricular design, graduation requirements, and the like are hotly debated. Finally, decision-making authority tends to be diffuse. Notably, who is really in charge of a given domain on campus is not always predictable from an organizational chart, and seemingly parallel or linked units and individuals may in fact rarely be in contact.

These notions are central to organization theorists' focus on "loose coupling" (Weick, 1976) and "anarchic" qualities (Cohen and March, 1974) in higher education. In such a setting, those theorists assert, there are multiple individual and organizational definitions of success, as well as multiple perceptions of how success might be measured. Obviously, these ambiguities will affect locally operational definitions of marginal productivity.

Of particular importance is the existence of multiple products of faculty labor. Beaumont (1985) and others have questioned the relevance of labor market theories to higher education on the grounds that, in a multiproduct service arena like higher education, labor input and output cannot be precisely quantified. Without such quantification, markets cannot rely on clear-cut assessments of productivity and therefore cannot sort the supply and demand of labor efficiently.

For our purposes, these conclusions by economists and organizational analysts boil down to a convincing litany of doubts about the likelihood of ever determining appropriate levels of compensation in higher education, either from the perspective of equity theory (in determining what is fair, how does one weigh contributions to different kinds of goals?) or from the perspective of labor market theory (what is marginal productivity in a context of shifting, debatable institutional priorities?).

Within-Unit Salary Dislocations Based in Time of Hire

In some university colleges and departments, faculty hired more recently receive salaries starkly different from comparable faculty hired in earlier years, because of rising or falling demand for their services in other institutions or organizations. Because of the declining fortunes of university medical schools, senior clinical faculty hired more recently have been offered pay lower than might have been expected in earlier years, and therefore have begun from smaller real base salaries than earlier cohorts (Mangan, 1996). As noted earlier, the opposite pattern ("salary compression") has emerged in business schools and some related fields: faculty hired more recently have been able to command higher salaries than their peers who have been on campus for years, because of increasing demand for their employment in other institutions and in the corporate sector. The phenomenon of widely differing salaries for faculty of similar productivity within academic units clearly involves a violation of horizontal equity, that is, the notion that those doing similar things similarly well should be paid similarly.

A number of recent studies have suggested that, when rank and other confounding factors are controlled, years employed on a given campus tend to be negatively associated with faculty salary levels (McCulley and Downey, 1993; Webster, 1995). While this pattern is no doubt partially caused by real merit differences among faculty, the pattern surely also reflects changing market conditions (Scott and Bereman, 1992). Snyder et al, 1992) have noted that problems of this kind may be expected to grow, and are worthy of serious institutional attention.[21]

Across-Unit Salary Dislocations Based in Differences in Fields' Internal and External Markets

Like the preceding phenomenon, the phenomenon of widely differing salaries for faculty of similar rank and productivity across academic units involves a violation of horizontal equity. Here, however, the tenet being violated is that those doing similar things similarly well in various parts of the campus should be paid similarly. External markets, and some internal dynamics as well, have produced salary profiles that vary notably by academic units. Differential performance across individual units does not seem to explain these differences. Faculty in some areas (e.g., engineering and business) are paid much more than similarly performing faculty elsewhere on campus. If one adopts the restrictions of traditional neoclassical theory, defining productivity uniformly across units (thus assuming a similar system of valuation in the internal marketplace and assuming a rather homogeneous external market for all professors), the higher salaries of some professors relative to other professionally comparable professors may not make sense. Clearly, there is no single internal or external marketplace for university professors. Instead, fields differ not only in the ways they evaluate productivity but also in the external labor markets they face.

Distinctively Different Salaries for Women

The fact that men and women of comparable abilities, performance, and other characteristics are sometimes rewarded differentially is an archetypal example of horizontal inequity. The American Association of University Professors (1992), after surveying existing scholarly literature as well as the consensus values of its members, has expressed its views on this problem:

> In the university context, differentials between and among departments on a given campus may be legitimate if they are the result of differences in the cost and length of required training, of off-campus possibilities for lucrative use of skills involved, or of the rarity of the necessary talent. Inequities in pay occur if the sex composition of a discipline affects faculty salaries, net of legitimate determinants of salary, or if tasks that are disproportionately assigned to female faculty members (e.g., teaching large service courses, advising students) are systematically underrewarded. That considerable sex segregation exists in academic institutions makes possible substantial pay inequity. (p. 33)

In this official statement, the AAUP combines equity theory and labor market theory to suggest that some differences in salaries between men and women are legitimate, but others may well not be. The association argues further that, within departments, the assignment of tasks tends to be gender-based and tends to disadvantage women in the contest for salaries. Such subtleties often are ignored in analyses of gender inequities in the literature. If gender is irrelevant to faculty members' productive capacity, then our focal theories would suggest it should also be irrelevant in the determination of their salaries. Such seems not to be the case.

Moderately Flat Salary Structures Across Fields

Although there are, as noted above, clear differences in salary levels across fields, these differences are not so great as those in the nonacademic world, according to a number of economists (e.g., see Freeman, 1979). Were academic salaries fully reflecting external markets, the range between, say, the salaries of business and philosophy professors would be far greater than it really is. In actuality, as Bowen and Schuster (1986) note, the potential salary differences are apparently muted by academe's internal values and norms. In concert with that view, Freeman (1979) argues that

> In essence, in place of market valuations, universities affirm an intellectual value structure that presupposes little or no inherent superiority to knowledge in various fields . . . . Faculty are judged by their intellectual quality and scholarly output, with differences in the market price of output (which is substantial between, say, economics and Hittite archeology) ignored as much as possible in determining wages. Underlying this rejection of market prices is the realization that valuation of knowledge involves considerable uncertainty, nonappropriability, or externalities and time horizons that may be inadequately handled by for-profit market prices. (p.72)

This middling level of by-field variation constitutes a violation of not only the strict labor market theory assumption that faculty operate in one labor market with consistent definitions of productivity and value but also the more relaxed assumption of other versions of the theory that, if differential salaries by field exist, differences in salaries will *fully* reflect differential market valuations by field. In other words, the existence of a moderate level of salary dispersion across fields may be what is least expected by labor market theory, but that is precisely what we find in higher education. As usual, realities are somewhat more complex than ideal-type theories suggest.

Freeman also notes that flat salary structures can be costly: equity is purchased at the cost of losing some faculty in externally advantaged fields, gaining surpluses of faculty in externally disadvantaged fields, losing flexibility in responding to labor market conditions, and relying heavily on costly nonsalary compensation to offset salary gaps in advantaged fields (e.g., quicker promotion periods, better working conditions, liberalized consulting regulations, provision of special professorial chairs, provision of expensive laboratories, and the like). In surplus fields, higher-quality faculty can be hired, while in shortage fields, faculty hires may be of lower quality. All these costs of flat salary structures are borne by institutions, Freeman argues, in the interest of maintaining internal value coherence and collegiality.

Absent outright salary interventions by central administrators, two factors can offset the tendency to flatness in salaries. First, "when faculties are divided by schools . . . as among law, business, medicine, and arts and sciences, pressures for wage equity across disciplines will be attenuated" (p. 72). Second, because efforts to keep salary structures flat are costly, they are likely to be loosened in times of financial stress. That is, when funds are tight, the flatness of salary structures may decrease, depending on where salary growth can be limited and where it must be speeded (ibid.).

Uniform Salary Increments

In many institutions and academic units, salary increments are awarded across the board; that is, all faculty receive essentially the same percentage raises (see Simpson, 1981; Beaumont, 1985; Hansen, 1988a). Bowen and Schuster (1986) defend the use of the acrosstheboard approach on the basis of its low costs (largely avoiding individualized assessments) and its benefits in preserving collegiality and the special nature of higher education. They express pleasure that, in most postsecondary institutions, individualized merit pay has tended to be minor, "simply a little whipped cream on the pie, if given at all" (p. 250). Economists William Becker and Darrell Lewis (1979) agree with Bowen and Schuster that screening for differential performance is uncomfortable for many faculty and administrators, but argue that it is ultimately no more expensive to institutions and is critical to giving faculty the appropriate expectation that "incremental productivity will be matched with incremental salary gains" (p. 309).

Whether one likes across-the-board raises or not, they clearly involve some significant deviations from equity and labor market theories. From those perspectives, choosing to adopt the across-the-board approach means choosing to ignore individual and unit differences in performance and thus differences in worth to the institution. Inequities and inefficiencies emerge and, simply put, the connection between salary and productivity is compromised.

The "Annuity Feature" of Salaries

Regardless of whether a salary system awards raises across the board or is more merit-centered, annual salary adjustments are usually awarded on the basis of percentages rather than raw dollar amounts. For this reason, awards are usually made independently of the base dollar salary (Hansen, 1988a). For example, there is rarely any formal consideration of the fact that a 3 percent raise for a faculty member earning $75,000 is $2,250, while for a faculty member earning $30,000 the same raise is only $900. Even under a strongly merit-centered system, a 3 percent merit raise for the higher-earning faculty member of the example would provide a greater raise in dollar terms than a 7 percent merit raise for the lower-earning faculty member. Ultimately, the nation's progressive income tax system will even this score somewhat in take-home pay, but the fact remains that the poorly performing but higher-paid faculty member would lose little if any economic ground to the high-performing but poorly paid faculty member. Under the normal ranges of faculty salary increments, it would take many years for the latter to catch up with the former, if indeed he or she ever would.

This phenomenon, which we introduced earlier in briefer form in our discussion of the effects of relative salaries, is an aspect of what is sometimes called the "annuity feature" of salaries. The phenomenon implies that early salary advantages tend to dissipate very slowly if at all, even in the face of superior performance by others (see Lawler, 1990).

If initial salary differences are based in inequities (e.g., in gender-based discrimination in salaries), the implications of the annuity feature are even more troubling. Lower initial salaries propel lower savings as well as lower contributions to pension funds. Year after year, funds lost through unjustified salary deficits could be compounding in a disadvantaged employee's investment account. Similarly, unjustly absent institutional matching funds for pensions could be compounding as well. Therefore, simply equalizing annual pay for a disadvantaged group at some midpoint in a career falls far short of truly evening the score. What is more, if unfairly low salaries are allowed to persist unameliorated throughout a working career, their effects do not end with the end of employment; they also eventually lead to lower retirement benefits, to the extent such benefits are based on final salary.

The annuity feature of academic pay contradicts the theoretical notions that salary changes should be tied closely to merit in both percentage and dollar terms and that existing salaries should reflect current rather than past worth to the organization. Academic compensation systems that add merit pay to base salaries in small percentage increments allow inequities to persist and sometimes grow. Faculty who have long ceased being top performers tend to have few outside offers, so they remain on campus where they continue to reap the financial advantages of their earlier successes. In contrast, unless special institutional funds are available for making strong counteroffers to faculty being wooed to go elsewhere, high performers who arrived early in their careers may be recruited away by those who can pay salaries better approximating their current worth on the marketplace.

Unfortunately, these fundamental problems are not easily solved. Alternatives to the annuity feature tend to be unattractive and tend themselves to be inconsistent with equity and labor market theories. For example, awarding lower merit raises (in dollar or percentage terms) to those with higher salaries in a unit, simply on the a priori basis of their initial salaries, seems contrary to the spirit of matching salary and current performance. Lawler (1990, p. 75), writing about salary systems in corporations as well as government settings, has argued that it is virtually impossible to have a salary system that both effectively motivates staff performance in the short term (via large annual merit-based raises) and retains the best performers over the longer term (via merit-based levels of overall compensation). The annuity feature of merit pay, in concert with the inevitability of limited resources, means one of these two goals has to be sacrificed. Either the best performers maintain the highest salaries and are retained by snagging most of the dollar raises, or performance is more generally motivated by significant raises for those lower in the salary structure.

In universities, boards and legislators have tended to impose formally the use of percentage rather than dollar increases in salaries and to avoid large individual salary changes from year to year. Effectively, this has meant limiting salary changes for the great majority of faculty to raises within a small percentage range (usually 2 to 6 percent). These policies tend to prevent higher-performing, lower-paid faculty from gaining much on lower-performing, higher-paid faculty. The policies also tend to disadvantage high-performing, higher-paid faculty stars, who may make themselves available for recruitment raids by other institutions. Under the annuity feature, initial salaries are crucial for future salaries, so dramatic salary advancement for faculty at any rank often depends upon a willingness to leave after obtaining a high (initial) salary offer elsewhere or at least upon the willingness of an employing institution to match a higher salary offer obtained elsewhere. The great majority of faculty have no outside offers, so for them, initial salaries continue to exert their ancestral holds on later salaries throughout the course of employment at an institution. Given the legal and cultural constraints on university salary policies, fully satisfying solutions to the problems generated by the annuity feature may be nonexistent.

POLICY CHOICES FOR SALARY STRUCTURES IN RESEARCH UNIVERSITIES

Both empirically and conceptually, salary structures in research universities frustrate simple explanations and simple solutions. Those interested in developing salary structures in nonunionized research institutions face a number of challenges in linking salaries and performance efficiently and equitably. Prominent among those choices are the following:

- De-emphasizing the external marketplace
- Adopting the core salary approach
- Seeking to have annual salary changes directly parallel annual performance
- Standardizing salaries in association with career ladders
- Questioning the statistical controls in studies of gender differences in salaries
- Decoupling merit evaluation for salary increases and faculty development efforts
- Emphasizing dollar rather than percentage increments
- Pursuing internal consistency in salary determination
- Welcoming faculty participation in determination of merit-based salary increases
- Facilitating public scrutiny of salaries
- Elevating teaching and public service as criteria for salary adjustments

Each of these 11 choices is examined in the pages that follow. Unqualified, straightforward recommendations are generally avoided in favor of critically balanced reviews of the choices as potential initiatives for institutions. Policy recommendations are rarely appropriate for every institution across the diverse U.S. higher education system and, not surprisingly, there are no discernible silver bullets for those interested in salary policy. Instead, the hope is that the reviews of the policy choices here will provoke useful discussion and, ultimately, policy development.[22]

Choice 1: De-emphasizing the External Marketplace

A fundamental aspect of salary policy is the choice of an underlying strategic stance regarding the role of the external marketplace in faculty salary structures. A number of the issues we have discussed in this chapter (including salary compression within fields, salary dispersion across fields, gender differences in salaries, and the willingness to make sizable retention counteroffers to current faculty being recruited by other institutions) involve dislocations driven by external markets. Some institutions may choose to de-emphasize the influences of the external marketplace on their internal salary structures, while others may choose to allow markets to profoundly shape their salary structures.

With the choice to embrace the external marketplace comes a willingness to accept sizable differences in salaries for individuals in different academic fields (and in concert the probability of substantial gender differences in salaries on campus) as well as notable similarities among salaries for differently ranked individuals in given fields. Implicit in embracing the marketplace, therefore, is the danger of disillusionment among faculty in less well-paying fields, among senior, immobile faculty in high-demand fields like business and engineering, and among women. Beyond the soft threat of disillusionment lies the additional harder threat of legal action on grounds of discrimination by women or others. Potentially offsetting these negatives are some possible benefits: embracing the external marketplace might allow institutions to attract more qualified faculty, allow certain faculty not to feel a need to seek outside compensation through consulting, and allow flexibility for competitive offers in certain fields.[23] As Bowen and Schuster (1986), note, this perspective is based in the idea that "money is the mainspring that powers the academic enterprise" (p. 253).

Bowen and Schuster also concisely state the counter arguments to this view: universities differ from free markets, and if money drives academic life, then people's desire to serve, students' desire to learn, the benefits of faculty collegiality, and other important virtues of academe will be compromised. From this perspective, they suggest, "salaries should be set according to the valuations of the academic community, not necessarily according to valuations of the outside world . . . . Any other arrangement . . . will impair collegiality, will convey mistaken academic values, will create a sense of injustice among faculty, and will damage morale" (p. 253). What is more, the argument for de-emphasizing the market holds that institutions cannot and should not be expected to respond to every change in the marketplace. For anyone, that rudderless and opportunistic vision of university life is troubling indeed.

To de-emphasize the marketplace, an institution could adopt a salary schedule based entirely in seniority, a system based entirely in consistent internal valuations of merit (independent of both fields and external markets), or some combination of these two orientations. Such approaches are more likely to satisfy faculty threatened by the invisible hand of the external marketplace working within the institution.[24] A heightened sense of internal community, especially in the humanities and other lower-paying fields like education and social work, may result. The institution that acts to de-emphasize the external marketplace in faculty salaries may also be serving the greater goal of equity for women, minorities, and those in fields with low external demand for Ph.D.'s. The benefits of de-emphasizing the marketplace therefore include not only the protection of certain enduring academic virtues and values but also the potential amelioration of specific salary equity concerns.

De-emphasizing the external marketplace entails, however, a willingness to risk faculty disaffection in fields that pay well in other institutions and in other kinds of organizations, such as government or business. The institution may also find it more difficult to hire in fields with high external demand. That is, if the equalizing effort leads to lowering salaries for faculty in higher-paying fields (rather than to raising salaries for faculty in lower-paying fields toward the level of those in higher-paying fields), faculty disaffection and attrition are likely consequences in the formerly favored areas. For these reasons, de-emphasizing the external marketplace can be quite risky to the fortunes of any institution embarking on that policy venture alone.

A consortium of strong institutions, however, can counteract the internal salary inequities generated by the demand for Ph.D.'s in corporations, the government, and other institutions. After all, patterns in salary inequities do not vary much by institution, and similar policy measures could work across a wide range of institutions. There would still be unknown labor market dislocations owing to the possible changes in the supply of new graduate students in the affected fields, but the attractiveness of the institutions involved in the market de-emphasis consortium might offset those problems somewhat.

It should be stressed that market de-emphasis need not, and should not, imply full-blown rejection of external markets. Most analysts see such a move as impractical and unwise. Even Bowen and Schuster (1986), who are generally quite distrustful of the influences of external markets, recognize the unavoidable importance of market valuations in higher education. They argue, therefore, for a salary policy falling a little short of fully de-emphasizing the external marketplace. Specifically, they suggest helping faculty retool in high-demand fields, allowing faster promotion (thus higher pay) for faculty in high-demand areas, restricting entry to some high-paying majors to allow faculty supply in those fields to meet the demand, and favoring faculty in high-demand fields in the awarding of supplemental earnings (such as summer teaching funds and internal research grants).

Nichols-Casebolt (1993) agrees with Bowen and Schuster regarding the dangers of external marketplace influences in higher-education salaries, arguing that "responding purely to market forces in an academic setting challenges fundamental values about equity and the merit of a given professor's work (p. 583). She also shares Bowen and Schuster's pragmatism, however, observing that the conjunction of continuing financial pressures in academe with continuing shortages of faculty in some areas essentially rules out fully ignoring external markets. As an institution considers the appropriate level of market responsiveness in salaries, she suggests, there should be inclusive deliberations among all faculty.

That recommendation seems eminently sensible: decisions concerning market adjustments in salaries, whatever their genesis and direction, should fully and meaningfully involve faculty from a variety of fields.[25] It seems no exaggeration to suggest that a stance toward market-based salary dislocations can be a core strategic issue for institutions. To fail to address it comprehensively and publicly is to court divisiveness and institutional decline.

Choice 2: Adopting the "Core salary" Approach

In response to growing financial pressures posed by managed care organizations and health reform legislation, a number of university medical schools have broken up a faculty member's traditional base salary into a "core" component that is guaranteed and a second component that is "flexible" or "at risk" (see Mangan, 1996). That is, a professor's current and future salaries are unbundled into a foundational component and a supplemental component based in the clinical or funded research revenues generated by the faculty member or his or her academic unit. While the first portion of salary is assured from year to year (i.e., "hard money"), the second varies annually depending on the financial resources the faculty member generates for the institution. Medical school salaries are too distinctive and too complex a topic to consider fully in this essay, but the core salary approach is now being considered in other fields, so some attention to the idea here may be useful.

The core salary idea is conceptually and legally linked to tenure. Tierney (1997b) notes:

> The assumption has long been that tenure is equivalent to an individual's base salary. Summer salaries and bonuses were negotiable, of course, but an individual fit within some form of a salary scale, and he or she was guaranteed that base. Recent arguments have called for tenure to be the equivalent of a portion of an individual's salary, but not 100% of it. That percentage may be as low as 20% of what the individual has come to think of base pay or as much as 90% . . . No one will receive full compensation. The expectation is that the individual, the department, the school, and the institution all need to work creatively to generate the additional income necessary to cover the salary—but it is not guaranteed (p.20).

The adoption of this approach in universities would represent a radical change. Under guidelines of the AAUP, salaries at an institution may be reduced across the board in conditions of financial exigency. Institutions have historically not been allowed to reduce the salaries of *individual* tenured faculty members, however, without the due process guaranteed by tenure. In reality, this has meant that, even when the salary reduction is for a clear-cut, academically justifiable cause, lengthy hearings and appeals have been required.[26] The new core salary approach, if approved by governance bodies of institutions and upheld by the courts, would mark the end of this traditional form of financial security for faculty. Individual salaries could be reduced far more easily.

Strengths of the core salary approach may include increasing the flexibility of institutions to move resources from one area to another (unproductive faculty are forced to adapt to fewer resources or leave) and encouraging individual initiatives toward generating external revenues. In addition, because faculty become responsible for generating income on their collective behalf, the approach may produce more cohesiveness in academic units (Tierney, 1997b). On the other hand, potential threats to faculty satisfaction and financial security are clear. The AAUP (1996), expressing fears that a trend toward the core salary approach might harm the financial well-being of many faculty, has recently reiterated its stand that tenure must ensure a salary adequate to the maintenance of economic independence.

Under certain conditions, both the first and second policy choices considered here could lead to lower salaries for faculty in higher-paying fields. In appearance, the two are opposed: the core salary option involves an embrace of the marketplace rather than a shunning of the marketplace. Yet, consider their typical end results under current conditions. Medical faculty's salaries were raised to high levels because of great demand for clinical faculty in an earlier era. They have stayed at those levels, despite severe cooling in that demand, because faculty salaries cannot easily be lowered. Attuning compensation to the current marketplace by adopting the core salary approach usually leads to lowered salaries. Administrators of medical schools have argued that the marketplace demand for clinically adept physicians was the basis for the higher salaries of their faculty in the first place and, therefore, "If the argument is good on the upside, it should be equally good on the downside."[27] That is, as the market for physicians softens, so should faculty salaries.[28] Extending this to other academic areas would mean tying salaries there to emerging conditions in those distinctive labor markets, whatever their conditions.

Similarly, as noted earlier, adopting a standard for faculty salaries that is *independent* of outside marketplace demands (the first option) most likely involves adopting an institution-wide pay scale tending to fall below that offered in the higher-paying fields, and thus lowering the salaries of faculty in those fields. The parallel in the results of the two seemingly opposite approaches (ignoring the market and adopting the market-centered core salary approach) arises because of the inability of current marketdriven salary systems to respond efficiently to labor markets on the downside. When those systems are in place in fields with declining real prices for labor, efficiency is compromised by the ossification of a given faculty member's salary at levels dictated by the higher-demand markets of earlier eras.

Choice 3: Seeking to Have Salary Changes Directly Parallel Annual Performance

The discussion of the core salary approach raises a more fundamental question for institutional salary policy: To what extent is an institution willing to live with the implications of true efficiency in salary determinations? In classic economic theory, efficient salary systems allow downward as well as upward movement in individual salaries, in response to variations in employee performance (worth to the organization). Universities, however, are reluctant to tolerate salary reductions, even when the marketplace suggests them. What is more, any system attuning pay to performance along some dimension creates wide salary advantages for those performing well, thereby compromising the flatness of salary structures. In short, efficiency in salary systems can mean dispersion in salary levels, and institutions have to decide whether, for them, that dispersion means unacceptable discomfort.

The above point reinforces the conclusion that the question of merit as a factor in salary raises more difficulties than one might at first suppose. Traditional perspectives from economics as well as management theory tie salaries as closely as possible to performance, suggesting a strong reliance on merit increases from year to year. But the reward and incentive function of salaries can be compromised not only by the annuity feature but also by the fact that sorting faculty members by individual performance can diminish morale and collegiality, especially among employees who are tenured, modestly productive, and have no other career options (Bowen and Schuster, 1986), by the fact that merit systems can provide openings for favoritism and discrimination, and therefore may result in legal challenges (Lee, 1989), and by the difficulties of defining and measuring merit in multiproduct organizations like universities (Tuckman, 1976).

Thus, there are plausible counterarguments to adopting an aggressive merit system in salaries. On the other hand, rigid salary schedules and standardized increments may reward underachievers equally to others, and may raise numerous other problems as well (Hansen, 1988a). Some balance is necessary. Certainly, if an institution is going to commit to a merit system, it should be willing to make aggressive adjustments to minimize the problems associated with the annuity feature and the other issues raised above. Even the most performance-oriented institution should be willing to consider systems that mix merit considerations with other approaches to awarding salaries.

Hansen (1988b) acknowledges that fully merit-driven systems tend to produce the closest ties between salaries and productivity but raise a number of difficulties. He therefore categorized percentage increment salary systems on the basis of their degree of acceptance of merit as a criterion in salary levels and evaluated those systems. As alternatives to fully merit-driven systems, he considers three other systems: (1) equal percentage raises for everyone, with no merit component (this tends to maintain a set salary structure, and may make it hard to recruit and retain faculty); (2) equal percentage raises for everyone, with a small allocation of additional funds to reward the special merit of some faculty members (this tends to make only small changes in salary structures); and (3) equal but small percentage increments for everyone, plus a large allocation of additional funds to reward merit (this tends to widen salary distributions over time).[29] For reasons discussed earlier, Hansen's first alternative to a pure merit system seems unacceptably inefficient: salary is fully uncoupled from individual performance. The second system is attentive mainly to professional maturity, rank, and cost-of living changes, while the third weighs merit more highly than those factors. While the second system can give administrators in largely standardized systems the flexibility to recognize faculty merit, it works mainly to preserve the institutional culture and community so highly prized by Bowen and Schuster (1986) and others.

A special area for attention in debates about merit pay is the possibility of negative salary adjustments. Pursuing such adjustments might encourage departure among the unproductive, even among unproductive tenured faculty. It might also create alienation without departure, however, among those faculty who have no career alternatives elsewhere. Faced with the cultural and legal constraints on salary reductions, Hansen (1985) suggests, administrators might more feasibly choose providing unproductive faculty with some combination of restricted real salary growth (i.e., salary raises under the rate of inflation) and positive incentives for improvement.

Choice 4: Standardizing Salaries in Association with Career Ladders

Most faculty work under the contract salary system, in which each faculty member negotiates a salary individually with a representative of the employing institution, usually the head of the home academic unit. A contrasting system is used in the military, government, K12 education, and in a few state systems of higher education: the standardized salary schedule (Simpson, 1981; Beaumont, 1985; Hansen, 1988a).[30] Such systems, when used in higher education, offer a single, officially specified salary for each academic rank and, usually, a standard time-in-step specification for each salary step. This approach imposes highly elaborated procedures and a regulated chain of command on salary determinations. Few research universities operate under standardized systems, but some analysts suggest the approach is gaining adherents (see, e.g. Bowen and Schuster, 1986).

A standardized approach can be tailored to accommodate a wide variety of independent salary schedules while at the same time offering clear-cut quantitative criteria for advancement in rank. The appearance of rigor (and thus of an absence of unwarranted subjectivity) may help gird such systems against internal disputes and legal challenges on equity grounds. Such systems can also be adapted for nontraditional employment arrangements, such as those differentiating research and teaching tracks and those featuring clinical professorships. Because standardized systems employ straightforward formulaic procedures for salary adjustments, they are often viewed as relatively inexpensive.

The establishment of a bureaucratized salary schedule does not necessarily imply a rejection of the external academic marketplace. An institution can create exceptions or special categories for faculty in fields with high salaries in external settings. For an example, consider the University of California's standardized but extraordinarily differentiated salary system (University of California System, 1996). There are six ranks at the assistant professor level. In 1996–97, Assistant 1 provided a nine-month annual salary of $39,600, while the salary for Assistant 6 was $51,500. There are five ranks at the Associate level and eight at the full Professor level (salaries for the latter ranging from $57,600 to $101,100 in 1996–97). Beyond these 19 formal ranks, pay differentials for different fields are allowed, and flexibility is also made possible by the system's provisions for off-scale salaries, negotiable for faculty at any level under certain circumstances. Although there are formal limits on the extent to which these negotiated nonscale salaries can vary from the official salary schedule, the UC System clearly allows substantial leeway for consideration of external markets in salary setting.

The risks of standardized salary systems merit close attention, however. Such systems can decouple salaries and performance, and thus can be inefficient as strategic human resource management tools (Becker and Lewis, 1979). Also worth considering are such systems' potential to reward mediocrity and simple survival over time in a position and their tendency to substitute easily quantifiable factors like time on task or seniority for more valid and reliable indicators of faculty productivity.

It is intriguing that both sides in the debate over standardized systems accuse the other of being more costly. Those favoring standardized salary schedules argue that the costs of merit determinations under individualized contract arrangements include not only financially burdensome administrative oversight and faculty review processes but also the risk of excessive subjectivity and inequities. On the other side, Becker and Lewis (1979) argue that costs are greater over the long term when faculty productivity is ignored or downplayed in salary systems. There is a high cost, they argue, to tolerating mediocrity. They also argue that "a solidly rationalized and carefully implemented" academic reward system can avoid some of the problems of highly standardized systems, such as bureaucratic rigidity, restricted access to decision makers, and faculty alienation (p.306).

Choice 5: Questioning the Statistical Controls in Studies of Gender Differences in Salaries.

Faculty salaries are determined by a variety of factors, and those factors tend to be associated with each other. Compared to male faculty, female faculty more often are located in lower-paying fields, more often take distinctive routes into their professorships, more often follow distinctive patterns once in their academic careers, more often are part of two-career couples, and more often are active in poorly rewarded activities on campus, such as committee service and undergraduate advising (Rosenfeld and Jones, 1987; McElrath, 1992; AAUP, 1997; Lee, Leslie, and Olswang, 1987; Fox, 1985). Furthermore, women have only in the past two decades entered academic positions at rates beginning to approximate their potential representations, so the senior ranks of most institutions and most fields are dominated numerically by men while women are more frequently represented in the lower-paying junior ranks (AAUP, 1996b).

Because gender is associated with so many aspects of academic careers, analysts must take special care when addressing salary inequities. Conclusions are critically dependent on the ways multivariate models take into account individual characteristics and marketplace characteristics. In statistical terms, this issue often boils down to debates over what kinds of "controls" are appropriate in regression models. Apparent salary inequities can shrink as more and more control variables are included in regression analyses. That is, *the broader one's acceptance of control factors in gender-oriented salary studies, the less inequitable the system may seem.* Importantly, the amounts designated for equity-based salary adjustments for women may tend to shrink as an institution accepts arguments for adding various control factors. But the very act of "taking these factors into account" can be viewed as a concession to existing inequities in the larger marketplace and in the structure of opportunity for academic women (AAUP, 1992). Careful scrutiny is warranted for some of the controls that reduce the salary gaps empirically specified in multivariate models.

Consider, as the most striking example, the case of field differences in salaries. Controlling for field-based salary differences removes much of the empirical difference in the salaries of male and female faculty, and makes institutions appear more equitable. Whether the gender distribution of faculty among different fields can be viewed as a *cause* of field differences in pay patterns or simply an artifact of a variety of societal and institutional considerations is a fundamental, and vexing, policy question. The latter interpretation calls for using field differences as controls, while the former questions that kind of control. Most analysts who have done sophisticated work in the area tend to agree with the AAUP that the gender composition of fields actually affects their faculty pay level (see AAUP, 1992). Proponents of this view argue that salary structures in which business faculty are paid one and a half times as much as languages faculty at comparable rank are not blameless on gender grounds. To argue otherwise, they suggest, is tacitly to endorse the larger society's differential marketplace valuations of people in those fields. Absent any compelling other reason for the salary differences between the fields, some faculty advocate that universities establish their own, independently generated and presumably more equitable standards for salaries in different fields.

Opponents of this view doubt the premise that gender composition actually affects salaries: the fact that female faculty are predominantly in fields paying less is simply artifactual of the ethically neutral workings of larger markets. Opponents also argue that, regardless of one's judgments of external marketplaces' valuations, it is unwise to tamper with such marketplaces because actively resisting the going level of salaries in fields can create labor shortages in some areas and oversupplies in others, especially in institutions seeking to make adjustments independently of other institutions (see the discussion of Choice 1 above).[31]

In the context of such disagreement, it is important to stress two things to policy makers. First, sophisticated quantitative analyses with ample controls are necessary for specifying the nature and extent of gender-based differentials on campus. Second, however, it is equally essential to remember that the success of such controls in reducing or removing evidence of gender differences does not imply that gender-based problems should be discounted. An inclusive definition of such problems, with skepticism toward claims of the gender neutrality of field-based salary differences and other control factors, seems essential for progress on this front.[32]

Choice 6: Decoupling Merit Evaluation for Salary Increases and Faculty Development Efforts.

Administrators often seek to reward productive faculty with merit-based salary raises and to improve faculty productivity through individually tailored development efforts. Both of these activities can involve peer observation, self-reporting, and the compilation of documentary evidence on the quality of faculty performance. Unfortunately, faculty's incentive to do well in salary evaluations can come into conflict with their incentive to improve the quality of their teaching, research, or service. That is, while the most desirable attitude toward faculty development efforts is a willingness to expose one's own weaknesses for evaluation by others, in the interest of improvement, the understandable attitude toward salary determinations is to present oneself in the best possible light, in the interest of higher pay. In the terms of evaluation research, one process (salary determination) is summative, while the other (faculty development) is formative. When departments confound the two processes, the potential for true faculty improvement may suffer.[33]

For example, faculty may resist or undermine a system of peer reviews of classroom teaching if that review has overlapping implications for salary determination and teaching improvement. Colleagues may be unwilling to review a peer negatively, especially a tenured peer who is apt to be a continuing colleague to the reviewers. Likewise, faculty being reviewed may try to influence reviews to focus upon their strengths and downplay areas of weakness (e.g., arranging classroom visits by reviewers to come on days with class discussion rather than lectures). Faculty development is facilitated by willingly exposing one's instructional weaknesses in the interest of improvement, but that behavior is unlikely when the financial stakes are high. The option of somehow decoupling merit evaluation for salary raises and faculty development efforts therefore seems to make sense.

One area in which the two might be distinguished relates to change. Two kinds of scores might be identified each year for each faculty member: measures of quality and measures of change in quality. For example, a faculty member might score low relative to peers in average student evaluations of teaching, but the gain in the professor's average scores from one year to the next might still be appreciable. While salary increases might be based on the average score, faculty development efforts might focus on the change. There are problems with this approach, however. For one thing, if change is the focus of formative evaluation but irrelevant for salary determinations, the financial rewards for improvement may be small in the short term: faculty who always do well in research or some other area and receive unchangingly high ratings in that domain might well receive higher salary increases than those who have worked hard to improve and shown some meaningful gains. Improvement is the ultimate goal of faculty development efforts, and should be reflected in salary gains as well.

There are, or should be, a number of direct parallels in the two kinds of evaluation. Both should certainly rely significantly on rigorous measurement. The emphases in salary reviews should be congruent with the emphases of faculty development efforts. Also, the emphases of both should reflect the larger mission of the unit. An unacceptably weak teacher may choose to ignore or avoid faculty development efforts in instruction in order to spend more time in research projects, if grant funding and publications associated with such projects are clearly the key to salary increases in his or her unit.[34] Any effort to uncouple reviews for salary and for faculty improvement must deal with the fact that the two should both be working toward the same ends, and will inevitably involve some overlap.

In the end, the two activities may be impossible to separate fully. In any but the largest academic units, the individuals involved in one area will often be the individuals involved in the other, or at least personally or organizationally close to those in the other area. Department chairs, in particular, will often be privy to information of both kinds, and influential in action on both fronts. It may require herculean psychic strength for a chair, or even associated committees with delegated responsibilities in the two arenas, to separate totally the two bodies of information.

The challenge, therefore, is to maintain the distinctive integrity of formative and summative evaluation of faculty as effectively as possible in the context of an integrated unit mission. One relatively simple step is to assure that, as Keig and Waggoner (1994) stress, "Institutional rewards and incentives should be structured to demonstrate to faculty that participation in formative peer evaluation . . . is truly valued" (p. ix).[35] Specifically, salary awards should reflect the emphasis on formative evaluation in the unit: those who reject the latter may suffer under the former. A second, more difficult step is to separate the activities of the two processes as fully as possible, understanding and accepting that there will be inevitable overlaps. As Keig and Waggoner (1994) argue, different but equally rigorous evaluation processes must be initiated and supported within units for purposes of salary determination and faculty development.

Choice 7: Emphasizing Dollar Rather Than Percentage Increments.

Although most institutions using merit-based systems award the best performers the highest percentage increments, many corporations award their best performers the highest dollar increments. These alternative approaches can provide strikingly different results. Consider a department in which the most productive faculty for the past year were in the lower-paying ranks. Under a percentage raise system, the highest dollar gains might well be among the weaker-performing faculty in the highest-paid ranks. Under a dollar raise system, the highest dollar and percentage gains would likely be among the higher-performing, lower-paid faculty.

Hansen (1988b) has argued that "awarding dollar increments usually reflects a desire to change the relative distribution of salary increases and hence alter (typically to narrow) overall salary differences among academic ranks and between lower and higher paid faculty members. Awarding percentage increments preserves the relative salary structure, which is viewed as essential in maintaining competitive salaries (p. 117). There may be reason to consider adopting dollar increments in some situations and in some faculty salary systems. Where there are substantial differences in salaries, where movement in the direction of lessening those differences is desired, and where institutions are willing to endure some market dislocations (see the earlier discussion of flat salary structures), dollar-based increments may make sense.

Choice 8: Pursuing Internal Consistency in the Determination of Salaries.

Burton Clark (1983), Karl Weick (1976), and others have observed that flexibility and decentralization are attractive features of university organization: allowing individual units to chart their own courses can contribute to institutional effectiveness. Nevertheless, some issues demand ongoing, aggressive central attention, and salary determination may well be one of those issues. When criteria and processes for salary advancement are allowed to shift over time and when there is substantial and uncontrolled across-unit variation in criteria and processes for salary advancement, women, minorities, and others may be disadvantaged (Fox, 1985). Fox suggests, "Without objective standards, functionally irrelevant attributes can govern evaluation to an appalling degree" (p. 422). For example, she notes that when units are left fully autonomous, putatively irrelevant factors like dress and politics can become elements in faculty evaluations. In a similar vein, Lee (1989) argues that central administrators need to conduct consistently designed, careful, regular, well-documented reviews of faculty performance to rebut assaults on merit pay and assure fairness.

Nevertheless, Lee, Fox, and many others have conceded that some flexibility in reward systems is necessary for academic units. For example, even in a research university, music is a field quite different from physics in its standard markers of scholarly success. Institutions must be wary of forcing one model unbendingly onto all fields, and should allow the criteria and processes for salary awards to vary at least marginally by field. Importantly, administrators should allow enough variation in departments' specific criteria for raises to assure that distinctive, strategically defensible departmental goals need not be abandoned in order to follow centralized institutional guidelines.

Choice 9: Welcoming Faculty Participation in Determination of Merit-Based Salary Increases.

There are benefits to a relatively democratic approach to awarding individual merit salary increases. When faculty are represented in the determination of salary changes at the unit level, decisions can be consensually legitimated, decision quality may be improved by the addition of multiple perspectives and new information, and administrators are somewhat more protected from charges of favoritism. An elected departmental salary advisory committee, for example, might buffer a merit-based system from charges of discrimination and lessen legal vulnerability. On the other hand, elected committees may not always reflect the core values of central or unit administrators. They may produce decisions that are more politically driven or more protective of certain interests or people than would be organizationally desirable from a purely strategic or purely economic perspective. What is more, privacy concerns can arise in some institutions unless the information provided to the elected faculty is appropriately screened.

In the end, the use of faculty participation in salary determination seems an approach best used contingently. When leaders are confident that those likely to be elected are in accord with core institutional values, or when leaders are unquestioningly willing to defer to the unit faculty, or when the role of committee members is circumscribed in managerially acceptable ways, such committees may make sense. There is no reason salaries should always be determined by administrators working alone.

Choice 10: Facilitating Public Scrutiny of Salaries.

The public visibility of salaries varies appreciably by unit and by institution. Openness about salaries often extends beyond faculty committees and beyond the level of academic units. In most public institutions, for example, faculty salaries are a matter of public record. Thus, the outcomes of salary determination processes are already available in many academic settings. Institutions vary in the ease with which such data may be accessed, however. It is important that policies concerning the visibility of salaries be thoughtfully designed.

Often, leaders are concerned that information about relative salary levels can lead to dissatisfaction. Hamermesh (1988), for example, has noted, "Some of the loudest complaints [by faculty members] are provoked by minute salary differences that upset previous wage equalities. Reducing access to this information by refraining from publicizing every last detail of salaries as widely as physically possible can prevent small random disturbances in the salary structure from generating immense dissatisfaction" (p. 24). Others have argued (see AAUP, 1992) that maintaining the confidentiality of salaries may spare faculty members from embarrassment.

Still, it is somewhat uncomfortable to argue, in a setting driven by democratic and scientific ideals, that professionals benefit from being deprived of information, especially information about something so fundamental. Institutions should at least consider making salary data more available to interested internal and external observers.

Some might take that injunction a step further. It seems a small step, at least conceptually, to make more public the *process* behind salary decisions. Although individual merit-salary determinations are usually considered part of the confidential personnel records of faculty, they have been accessed in court cases. Some analysts with an interest in gender equity on campus have argued for lessening the secrecy behind salary determination processes because doing so may also serve to remove the cover under which discriminatory decisions are made (AAUP, 1992). Of course, such a move raises potential legal and personnel problems, but the idea of publicizing salary determination processes under controlled circumstances seems worth additional consideration.

Choice 11: Elevating Teaching and Public Service as Criteria for Salary Adjustments.

A consistent analytic conclusion regarding salary determination in research universities is that research accomplishments are the primary factor in salary awards. Beyond some minimal level of competence, teaching and service seem clearly to play lesser roles in salary determination (Fairweather, 1996). One reason for this pattern is the fact that research productivity is often said to be easier to measure than success in teaching or service (see Tuckman, 1976). Of course, the absence of precise measurement is not, in and of itself, sufficient reason for disregarding nonresearch factors in salaries. In fact, the core values of research universities have emphasized research and downplayed the significance of service and teaching, thereby encouraging light regard for the latter activities in reward systems.

Recent years have brought some reconsideration of the primacy of research in university life (Boyer, 1990; Rice, 1996). This movement might well be helping reconfigure contemporary salary structures in the direction of more attention to teaching and service. Beyond the philosophical rationale for such a move lies some pragmatic reasoning. Societal and political pressures on higher education are trending toward more attention to teaching (Hearn, 1992). In addition, administrators may have some practical interest in elevating teaching. Blau (1973) suggested that "a faculty interested in research and capable of making research contributions has bargaining power that enables it to demand freedom from domination by centralized authority and to command greater influence in academic affairs as well as higher salaries" (p. 169). Conversely, a faculty more interested in teaching is likely to be more dependent on local funding and thus on administrator approval (as opposed to approval by funding agencies and peers). As Lewis (1996) has noted with some asperity:

> Those who work hard at teaching and approach it with idealistic devotion are entrapped. If one's scholarship dwindles, one's marketplace value becomes nil. In effect, those whose sole focus is on teaching become hostages to the institution where they work. Academic administrators would have some interest in this eventuality. Having faculty engaged in teaching at the expense of disciplinary matters gives institutional authorities more control over them. One would expect faculty with fewer career options to be more compliant (p. 145).

Nevertheless, it is unclear how well internal and external authorities will be able to succeed in elevating teaching through reforms in salary systems. Faculty in research universities have been socialized, recruited, hired, and promoted within institutions in which research ruled the reward system. They may work effectively through governance mechanisms to thwart recasting of reward systems. Further, they may resist changing their behaviors even in the face of a revised salary system that more fully recognizes good teaching. After all, as noted earlier, there is no evidence that salary is a primary motivator of faculty behavior. In short, moving the research-oriented organizational culture in another direction via the salary system may be quite difficult.

JUDGING FACULTY SALARY STRUCTURES

Thoughtful choices along the dimensions outlined above are important to the effectiveness of institutional salary structures. Also important to effectiveness is thoughtful attention to some broader criteria on which *any* salary system should be judged. Eight such criteria are suggested here.

First, is the system efficient? That is, does it take an appropriate level of time or other resources to operate? Good training, effective communication, and appropriate oversight are among the features of a minimally wasteful system. Second, are the procedures for salary determination equitable? Do affected parties have some role in the process, for example? Third, are the outcomes of salary determination equitable for those in different fields, for those senior faculty suffering unduly from the effects of salary compression, for women, and for racial/ethnic minorities? Fourth, is the salary system well understood on campus and, as necessary, beyond the campus? Fifth, does the system allow adequate flexibility in response to potential policy crises and special cases? Sixth, does the system fit with the strategic initiatives, management approach, and organizational culture of the campus? Seventh, does the system make sense from an internal political perspective? That is, does it balance the interests of various parties on campus and reflect current political realities there? Eighth, is the system assessed and evaluated on a regular basis?[36]

As suggested by earlier discussion, judging how well a salary structure deals with questions of salary equity for female faculty can be especially complex, and may lead to conflicts among the above criteria.[37] For example, the route to equitable salaries for women may not be entirely compatible with participatory decision making in certain units, if gender equity is not valued in those units. Relatedly, the costs of achieving salary equity may be greater than some are willing to accept from an efficiency perspective. One of the most difficult salary-related challenges for leaders in academic settings is operationally defining outcome equity, procedural equity, and efficiency, and then determining appropriate trade-offs between these three desired outcomes.[38] In the end, the question of judging salary systems becomes thickly intertwined with institutional culture and individual values.

CONCLUSIONS

Salaries are only one piece in a mosaic of elements comprising the environment for faculty productivity. More fundamental than the adoption of any of the specific policies and evaluation criteria introduced above is the thoughtful consideration of broader institutional values and strategy. What are the most important equity, effectiveness, and efficiency issues on this campus? What kinds of financial and nonfinancial solutions are most acceptable? What should be the driving principles behind an institution's faculty reward systems, as they relate not only to salary but also to tenure, promotion, and other rewards? How should the institution's mission and core culture shape reward systems?

Only in this wider context is the recent increase in public, legislative, and administrative attention to salaries justifiable, and only in this context can effective salary policy be developed. Alone, salaries are neither the most important motivators for faculty in research universities nor the most uplifting of topics for those who view academe through a transformative lens. A single-minded focus on reforming salary policy alone, without consideration of its place in larger institutional concerns, makes little sense.

Yet, a single-minded focus on reforming faculty reward systems without close attention to salaries makes equally poor sense. To ignore salaries is to ignore not only a critical factor in institutional budgets and a central element in public critiques of higher education but also a noteworthy element in professors' feelings of satisfaction and productivity. Indeed, from an administrative perspective, salaries have the advantage of relative concreteness compared to the other factors in the motivational context surrounding professors. An academic leader may find it virtually impossible to learn about, much less influence, the scholarly work schedule or interests of a tenured professor, but he or she *can* change relatively more easily the ways in which that professor is financially rewarded. Here, at least *marginal* administrative influence on senior faculty performance seems possible. Salaries may be secondary to other factors in the reward context affecting senior professors, but they tend to be notably more measurable and manipulable than those other factors.

The problems in faculty salaries are significant. The opportunities for developing more effective salary policies are real. Salaries' potential as a lever for changing faculty behavior is perhaps more significant than many observers realize. Institutions' futures are highly dependent on their salary structures. In those four simple observations lies ample reason for academic leaders to focus energetically on the topic.

NOTES

This is a revised version of an invited paper prepared for the Center for Higher Education Policy Analysis, School of Education, University of Southern California. The author appreciates the research assistance of James Eck and the helpful comments of Bill Tierney and Susan Frost.

    1. An example in Sykes (1988) contention that some professors at the University of Michigan "are paid nearly $1000 an hour for their contact with

students" (p.40). The essay by Laing (1995) also reflects the problem. The cover graphic for that article, which appeared in *Barron's* weekly, is a cartoonish depiction of a complacent, arrogant professor dressed in fur-lined academic regalia and tightly clutching a sizable wad of cash.

2. For reasons of space, the chapter does not consider at any length the salaries of part-time faculty, graduate student instructors, clinical faculty, and adjunct faculty. Also little examined here are elements of faculty compensation beyond the standard academic contract. Finally, the chapter does not much consider questions relating to faculty unions and collective bargaining, which are rare in research universities.

3. In 1905, for example, Andrew Carnegie noted that college faculty were "the least rewarded of all professions" (Bowman, 1938, p. 57). Carnegie allocated funds for pensions to faculty to address the problem, however, and some colleges in the period began to offer health insurance and paid sabbatical leaves for travel, study, and research (Brubacher and Rudy, 1976).

4. Cited in Rudolph (1990, p. 196). Not all presidents of the period were so positive on the subject, however. In 1893, President William Rainey Harper of the University of Chicago lamented that faculty salaries were similar to those of skilled mechanical laborers, clerical staff, and railroad workers (Bowman, 1938).

5. In private institutions, that secrecy continues largely unabated (Burke, 1988). Many analysts have worried that this traditional secrecy helps inequities in salary levels endure (Caplow and McGee, 1958; Burke, 1988).

6. On non research campuses, union-affiliated faculties have tended to earn higher salaries (Lillydahl and Singell, 1993). Interestingly, however, salaries of faculties on the few unionized research university campuses in the 1980s tended to be lower than those of faculty on similar but nonunionized campuses, all else equal (ibid.). That finding may be a result less of some negative influence of unions than of the reluctance of faculties at the highest-paying, "elite" research institutions to unionize.

7. In a similar vein, Bowen and Schuster (1986) emphasize that faculty pay is relatively low because academic life is viewed as a "vocation" with solid nonmonetary rewards.

8. In a recent survey, administrators in public research-doctoral universities were far more likely than their peers in other institutions to perceive problems in the adequacy of faculty compensation on their campuses (American Council on Education, 1996). Interestingly, administrators in private research-doctoral universities were the least likely to report such problems.

9. These data are for all four-year institutions rather than for research universities alone, so inferences for the latter group should be made cautiously.

10. Ideally, one could easily examine longitudinal data for research university faculty disaggregated by both field and institutional control. This would allow comparisons, for example, of patterns in salaries for full professors of physics in private and public doctoral universities. Unfortunately, most easily accessible, recent data are cross-sectional, are aggregated on either control or field, are aggregated across institutional types, or exhibit some combination of those characteristics. Still, some useful inferences can be made.

11. From a survey by the College and University Personnel Association, reported in the *Chronicle of Higher Education* ("Engineering and Accounting," 1995).

12. It should be noted that the absence of change in overall female-male earnings ratios does not necessarily imply that there have been no improvements in the equity of hiring or remuneration processes in individual cases.

13. Recently, at Illinois State, some female professors withdrew from a gender equity dispute over salaries because they saw the differences on that campus as based in market differences. As a female associate professor of marketing commented, "The salary differential is based solely upon principles of economics—supply and demand" (Wilson, 1996, p. A11).

14. Some tentative evidence is available on the question. In a multivariate study using national data, Fairweather (1996) found that minority status was unrelated to salaries in research and doctoral institutions.

15. A far more fundamental policy challenge is the recruitment of talented minority undergraduates into graduate work (Breneman, 1988).

16. HERI surveys full-time college faculty who have at least some involvement with undergraduate teaching. Unfortunately, data on this particular question are not broken down by institutional type, so we cannot isolate the responses of university faculty alone.

17. To place units this way, they suggest analysts explore middle-range theories such as Biglan's (1973) categorizing of academic fields along the hard-soft, pure-applied, and life-nonlife dimensions.

18. Of special interest is his finding that minority status interacted with fields in determining salaries in the fine arts: minorities received higher salaries than nonminorities in those fields, in the context of controls for publications, institutional characteristics, teaching loads, and other factors.

19. This is known as the "annuity" problem in salaries. The issue is revisited later in this chapter.

20. Obviously, only caricatures of those theories can be presented here. As ideas are presented, however, analysts who have studied the issues in more depth are cited.

21. Their thoughts on the prospects for substantive amelioration are not optimistic, however. The complexities of the issue, and the evolving and unpredictable marketplace for doctorally trained personnel, make policy options difficult at best.

22. Others have also explored these choices productively. For especially useful discussions, see Becker and Lewis (1979); Fox (1985); Bowen and Schuster (1986); Hansen (1988a, 1988b); and Moore and Amey (1993).

23. William Tierney (personal communication, May 5, 1997) has noted the unattractiveness with letting other, nonacademic settings determine the worth of someone to an institution: "Basically, we tell someone 'go to another culture and have them value you. If they like you, then we will raise your salary' It really depresses the value of our own culture when we do it."

24. It should be noted that shunning the external marketplace does not necessarily mean shunning the internal marketplace, allowing salaries to vary, based on merit, within the institution and within departments. Indeed, assuming a common "production function" and thus a common system of differentiating rewards among employees across fields, is fundamental to traditional views of academic life (Bowen and Schuster, 1986).

25. Hamermesh (1988) discusses this view and raises some caveats.

26. Professor Parker Young (personal communication, December 18, 1996) has noted this often comes as a disappointing shock to external observers and trustees expecting quick results on productivity and cost cutting initiatives.

27. The comment is by David R. Perry, senior associate dean of the medical school at the University of North Carolina at Chapel Hill (cited in Mangan, 1996, p. A18).

28. A critical issue in the responsiveness and stability of salaries under this new system is the availability of "bridging" salary funds to smooth transitions for faculty whose grants have ended but who are preparing new research-funding proposals. Without such funds, the salaries of even the most entrepreneurially productive faculty could vary appreciably from year to year.

29. For a similar typology, see Simpson (1981).

30. Beaumont (1985) estimated that about one-third of U.S. institutions used such a system in the 1980s. The best- known examples may be those used in the mammoth public systems in California.

31. Proponents and opponents of gender-based adjustments tend to agree that coordinated efforts to address gender inequities *across* institutions stand a better chance of producing noteworthy changes while not creating painful dislocations in certain fields.

32. For useful discussions of the complexities of gender-based analyses of salaries, plus some thoughtful potential solutions, see Lee et al. (1987), Moore

(1993), and Balzer et al. (1996). It is important to note that most of the literature on gender differences in salaries focuses on the individual faculty member as the unit of analysis. Some additional insights may be gained from literature framed at the institution level. In such an analysis, Tolbert (1986) found that the most prestigious and selective institutions tended to hire more males than other institutions and pay them more. Relatedly, she found that institutions with small proportions of female faculty evidenced more gender discrimination in salaries.

33. Keig and Waggoner (1994) discuss this conflict in the context of instruction, in particular, but it has implications for developmental reviews of service and research activities as well.

34. For discussions of this conflict, see Tuckman (1976), Hearn (1992), and Fairweather (1996).

35. Whitman and Weiss (1982) note that "faculty evaluation will serve the dual purposes of making personnel decisions and developing faculty where it is rewarding in the PRT [promotion/retention/tenure] process for faculty to demonstrate evidence of development and improvement" (p.32).

36. See Becker and Lewis (1979), Moore and Amey (1993), and Stewart, Dalton, Dino, and Wilkinson, (1996) for useful examinations of some of these issues.

37. Noting these difficulties, the Commission on Women of the American Council on Education suggests that the criteria for salary decisions, the process for making decisions, and actual salaries, should be matters of public record. And, that all new employees should be informed as to how salaries are determined, that institutions should conduct and act aggressively upon salary equity reviews, and that campuses establish mechanisms to ensure that the principle of equal pay is incorporated in each round of salary decisions (Moses, 1996).

38. The difficulty of determining amounts for gender equity salary increments is a prominent example.

REFERENCES

American Association of University Professors (AAUP). (1992, July–August). Salary-setting practices that unfairly disadvantage women faculty. *Academe, 78* (4), 32–35.

―――. (1996a, January–February). Tenure in the medical school. A report of AAUP Committee A. *Academe, 82* (1), 40–45.

―――. (1996b, March–April). Not so bad. *Academe, 82* (2), 14–22.

―――. (1997, March–April). Not so good. *Academe, 83* (2), 12–88.

American Council on Education, (1996). *Campus trends.* Washington, DC

Balzer, W., Boudreau, N., Hutchinson, P., Ryan, A.M., Thorsteinson, T., Sullivan, J., Yonker, R., and Snavely, D. (1996). Critical modeling principles when testing for gender equity in faculty salary. *Research in Higher Education, 37,* 633–658.

Beaumont, M.S. (1985). *Salary systems in public higher education: A microeconomic analysis.* New York: Praeger.

Becker, W.E. (1985). Maintaining faculty vitality through collective bargaining. In S.M. Clark and D.R. Lewis (Eds.), *Faculty vitality and institutional productivity: Critical perspectives for higher education* (pp. 198–223). New York: Teachers College Press, Columbia University.

Becker, W.E., and Lewis, D.R. (1979). Adaptability to change and academic productivity. In D.R. Lewis and W.E. Becker, (Eds.) *Academic rewards in higher education* (pp. 299–312). Cambridge, MA: Ballinger.

Bellas, M.L. (1997). Disciplinary differences in faculty salaries: Does gender bias play a role? *Journal of Higher Education, 68,* 299–321.

Biglan, A. (1973). Relationships between subject matter characteristics and the structure and output of university departments. *Journal of Applied Psychology, 57* (3), 204–213.

Blau, Peter M. (1973). *The organization of academic work.* New York: Wiley.

Bowen, H.R., and Schuster, J. (1986). *American professors: A national resource imperiled.* New York: Oxford University Press.

Bowen, W., and Sosa, J. (1989). *Prospects for faculty in the arts and sciences.* Princeton, NJ: Princeton University Press.

Bowman, C.C. (1938). *The college professor in America: An analysis of articles published in general magazines, 1880–1938.* Philadelphia: University of Pennsylvania.

Boyer, C., and Lewis, D.R. (1984). Faculty consulting: Responsibility or promiscuity? *Journal of Higher Education, 55,* 637–59.

Boyer, Ernest L. (1990). *Scholarship reconsidered: Priorities of the professoriate.* Princeton, NJ: Carnegie Foundation for the Advancement of Teaching.

Breneman, D.W. (1988). Research on academic labor markets: Past and future. In D.W. Breneman and T.I.K. Youn (Eds.), *Academic labor markets and careers* (pp. 200–207). New York: Taylor and Francis.

Brown, David. (1965). *The market for college teachers.* Chapel Hill, NC: University of North Carolina Press.

Brubacher, J.S., and Rudy, W. (1976). *Higher education in transition: A history of American colleges and universities, 1636–1976.* New York: Harper and Row.

Burke, D.L. (1988). *A new academic marketplace.* New York: Greenwood Press.

Caplow, T., and McGee, R.J. (1958). *The academic marketplace.* New York: Basic Books.

Chronicle of Higher Education Almanac. 43 (1). (1996, September 2).

Chronicle of Higher Education. Engineering and accounting professors earn most, survey finds. (1995, April 28). *41* (33), A46–47.

Clark, Burton R. (1983). *The higher education system.* Berkeley, CA: University of California Press.

———. (1987). *The academic life: Small worlds, different worlds.* Princeton, NJ: Carnegie Foundation for the Advancement of Teaching.

Clotfelter, C.C. (1996). *Buying the best: Cost escalation in elite higher education.* Princeton, NJ: National Bureau of Economic Research.

Cohen, M., and March, J. (1974). *Leadership and ambiguity.* New York: McGrawHill.

College and University Personnel Association. (1995). *National faculty salary survey by discipline and rank in public colleges and universities.* Washington, DC: College and University Personnel Association.

Dillon, K.E., and Marsh, H.W. (1981). Faculty earnings compared with those of nonacademic professionals. *Journal of Higher Education, 52,* 615–623.

Fairweather, J.S. (1996). *Faculty work and public trust: Restoring the value of teaching and public service in American academic life.* Needham Heights, MA: Allyn and Bacon.

Fox, M.F. (1985). Publication, performance, and reward in science and scholarship. In J.C. Smart (Ed.), *Higher education: Handbook of theory and research.* (Volume1, pp. 255–282). New York: Agathon.

Freeman, Richard. B. (1975). Supply and salary adjustments to the changing science manpower market: Physics, 1948–1973. *American Economic Review, 65,* 27–39.

———. The job market for college faculty. In D.R. Lewis and W.E. Becker, (Eds.) *Academic rewards in higher education* (pp. 63–103). Cambridge, MA: Ballinger.

Hamermesh, D.S. (1988). Salaries: Disciplinary differences and rank injustices. *Academe, 74* (3), 20–24.

Hansen, L. (1985). Changing demography of faculty in higher education. In S.M. Clark and D.R. Lewis (Eds.), *Faculty vitality and institutional productivity: Critical perspectives for higher education* (pp. 27–54). New York: Teachers College Press, Columbia University.

———. (1988a). Merit pay in structured and unstructured salary systems. *Academe, 74* (6), 10–13.

———. (1988b). Merit pay in higher education. In D.W. Breneman and T.I.K. Youn (Eds.), *Academic labor markets and careers* (pp. 114–137). New York: Taylor and Francis.

Hearn, J.C. (1992). The teaching role of contemporary American higher education: Popular imagery and organizational reality. In W.E. Becker and D.R. Lewis (Eds.), *The economics of American higher education* (pp. 17–68). Boston: Kluwer.

Hearn, J.C., and Anderson, M.S. (1998). Faculty demography: Exploring the effects of seniority distributions in universities. In J.C. Smart (Ed.), *Higher education: Handbook of theory and research* (Vol. 13, pp. 235–273). New York: Agathon.

Katz, David A. (1973). Faculty salaries, promotions, and productivity at a large university. *American Economic Review, 63,* 469.

Keig, L., and Waggoner, M.D. (1994). *Collaborative peer review: The role of faculty in improving college teaching.* ASHE-ERIC Higher Education Report No. 2. Washington, DC: School of Education and Human Development, George Washington University.

Laing, J.R. (1995, November 27). Campus unrest. *Barron's,* pp. 25–26, 28–29.

Lawler, E.E. (1990). *Strategic pay: Aligning organizational strategies and pay systems.* San Francisco: JosseyBass.

Lawler, J.J., and Walker, J.M. (1980). Interaction of efficacy, commitment, and expectations in the formation of faculty attitudes toward collective bargaining. *Research in Higher Education, 13,* 99–114.

Lee, Barbara A. (1989). Academic personnel policies and practices: Managing the process. In G.G. Lozier and M.J Dooris (Eds.), *New directions for institutional research.* (No. 63, Managing Faculty Resources, pp. 3–18). San Francisco: Jossey-Bass.

Lee, Barbara A., Leslie, D.W., and Olswang, S.G. (1987). Implications of comparable worth for academe. *Journal of Higher Education, 58,* 609–628.

Lewis, Lionel S. (1996). *Marginal worth: Teaching and the academic labor market.* New Brunswick, NJ: Transaction.

Lillydahl, J.H., and Singell, L.D. (1993). Job satisfaction, salaries, and unions: The determination of university faculty compensation. *Economics of Education Review, 12,* 233–243.

Magner, D.K. (1997). Increases in faculty salaries fail to keep pace with inflation. *Chronicle of Higher Education, 43* (43), A8.

Mangan, Katherine S. (1996, July 26). Medical schools are reining in the salaries of faculty members. *Chronicle of Higher Education, 42* (47) A16, 18.

Marsh, J.F., Jr. and Stafford, F.P. (1967). The effects of values on pecuniary behavior: The case of academicians. *American Sociological Review, 32,* 747.

McCulley, W.L., and Downey, R.G. (1993). Salary compression in faculty salaries: Identification of a suppressor effect. *Educational and Psychological Measurement, 53,* 79–86.

McElrath, K. (1992). Gender, career disruption, and academic rewards. *Journal of Higher Education, 63,* 269–281.

McKeachie, W.J. (1979). Perspectives from psychology: Financial incentives are ineffective for faculty. In D.R. Lewis and W.E. Becker (Eds.), *Academic rewards in higher education* (pp. 3–20). Cambridge, MA: Ballinger.

McPherson, M.S., and Winston, G.C. (1988). The economics of academic tenure: A relational perspective. In D.W. Breneman and T.I.K. Youn (Eds.), *Academic labor markets and careers* (pp. 174–199). New York: Taylor and Francis.

Moore, K.M., and Amey, M.J. (1993). *Making sense of the dollars: The costs and uses of faculty compensation.* ASHE-ERIC Higher Education Report No. 5. Washington, DC: George Washington University.

Moore, Nelle. (1993). Faculty salary equity: Issues in regression model selection. *Research in Higher Education, 34,* 107–126.

Moses, Yolanda. (1996, December 12). Salaries in academe: The gender gap persists. *Chronicle of Higher Education, 44* (16), A60.

Newman, John Henry. (1996). *The idea of a university.* New Haven, CT: Yale University Press.

NicholsCasebolt, Ann M. (1993). Competing with the market: Salary adjustments and faculty input. *Research in Higher Education, 34,* 583–601.

Poisoned Ivy?: Academe is closely watching Minnesota's attack on tenure. (1996, June 10). *Business Week,* p. 40.

Rice, R. Eugene. (1996). *Making a place for the new American scholar.* Inquiry No.1, of Working Paper Series, "New Pathways: Faculty Careers and Employment for the 21st Century, a project of the American Association for Higher Education.

Rosenfeld, R., and Jones, J.A. (1987). Patterns and effects of geographic mobility for academic men and women. *Journal of Higher Education, 58,* 493–515.

Rudolph, F. (1990). *The American college and university: A history.* Athens, GA: University of Georgia Press.

Sax, L., Astin, A., Arredondo, M., and Korn, W. (1996, September). *The American college teacher: National norms for the 1995–96 HERI Faculty Survey.* Los Angeles: Higher Education Research Institute, University of California.

Scott, J.A., and Bereman, N.A. (1992). Competition versus collegiality: Academe's dilemma for the 1990s. *Journal of Higher Education, 63,* 684–698.

Simpson, W.B. (1981). Faculty salary structure for a college. *Journal of Higher Education, 52,* 219–236.

Smart, J.C. (1991). Gender equity in academic rank and salary. *Review of Higher Education, 14,* 511–526.

Smart, J.C., and McLaughlin, G.W. (1978). Reward structures in academic disciplines. *Research in Higher Education, 8,* 39–55.

Snyder, J.K., McLaughlin, G.W., and Montgomery, J.R. (1992). Diagnosing and dealing with salary compression. *Research in Higher Education, 33,* 113–124.

Stewart, K.D., Dalton, M.M., Dino, G.A., and Wilkinson, S.P. (1996). The development of salary goal modeling. *Journal of Higher Education, 67,* 555–576.

Sykes, Charles. (1988). *Profscam.* New York: St. Martin's Press.

Tarrant, L.L. (1996, October). *Ten-year trends for average faculty salaries.* Paper presented at the annual meeting of the Southern Association of Institutional Research and the Society for College and University Planning, Mobile, AL.

Tierney, W.G. (1997a, May 5.) Personal communication with the author.

Tierney, W.G. (1997b). Tenure and community in academe. *Educational Researcher, 26* (8), 17–23.

Tierney, W.G., and Bensimon, E.M. (1996). *Promotion and tenure: Community and socialization in academe.* Albany, NY: State University of New York Press.

Tolbert, P.S. (1986). Organizations and inequality: Sources of earnings differences between male and female faculty. *Sociology of Education, 59,* 227–235.

Tuckman, H.P. (1976). *Publication, teaching, and the academic reward structure.* Lexington, MA: Lexington Books.

U.S. Department of Education, (1990). *1988 National Survey of Postsecondary Faculty: Faculty in higher education institutions, 1988.* Washington, DC: U.S. Department of Education.

———. (1996). *Digest of education statistics.* Washington, DC: U.S. Department of Education.

University of California System, (1996, September 23). *Faculty—Ladder Ranks—Professor Series, Academic Year.* Report of the University of California System, Office of the President. Berkeley, CA: University of California System Office.

Webster, A.L. (1995). Demographic factors affecting faculty salary. *Educational and Psychological Measurement, 55,* 728–735.

Weick, K. (1976). Educational organizations as looselycoupled systems. *Administrative Science Quarterly, 21* (1), 1–19.

Whitman, N., and Weiss, E. (1982). *Faculty evaluation: The use of explicit criteria for promotion, retention, and tenure.* AAHE-ERIC Higher Education Research Report No. 2. Washington, DC: American Association for Higher Education.

Wilson, Robin. (1996, November 8). 350 female faculty members join a pay-equity dispute at Illinois State U. *Chronicle of Higher Education, 44* (11), A10–11.

Young, Parker (1996, Dec. 18). Personal communication with the author.

Young, Peyton A. (1994). *Equity in theory and practice.* Princeton, NJ: Princeton University Press.

CHAPTER 6

Talking Tenure
Opening Up the Conversation

Yvonna S. Lincoln
Texas A&M University

A CONVERSATION ABOUT TENURE

Higher education has found itself at the center of a conversation, a particularly bitter, querulous, and strident argument. Virtually every segment of American life has joined in the shouting match, and each has an opinion (whether or not particularly informed) regarding the issue. And unlike other crises that have confronted higher education since the end of the last World War, this one neither encounters a social solution nor does it appear that it will go away without major intervention. Of all the controversies, stresses, and financial strains to have assaulted higher education in the last half of the twentieth century, none appears to be so fraught with both bitterness and import as the issue of tenure. And no issue is likely to make such a profound and lasting impact on institutions of higher education (IHEs) as this issue.

Higher education accommodated the surging enrollments of the post-WWII returning veterans, and then faced again, with zest, the even more swiftly burgeoning enrollments of the children of those veterans, the so-called baby boomers. Not without pain, but nevertheless with remarkable stability, institutions weathered the program discontinuations and departmental closings of the late 1970s. Having argued for steady increases in faculty numbers throughout the 1950s and 1960s due to increasing enrollments, institutions found themselves hard-pressed to request continuing expansion when enrollments declined, and consequently, faculty numbers and ranks and programs shrank at some institutions (although decreasing faculty numbers and program closings affected far fewer institutions than media reporting would lead a general readership to believe). Institutions likewise adjusted curricula to meet the increasing vocationalism of a generation of students less interested in the liberal arts, and more interested in business, engineering, and computers. And again, institutions survived the criticisms of both right and left politics as they weathered the attacks on political correctness, a liberal arts curriculum that was the center of a "culture wars" controversy (Graff, 1992; Bromwich, 1992; Gross and Levitt, 1994; D'Souza, 1991; Bloom, 1987), and arguments in the courts regarding who shall be admitted, and by what criteria (Lucas, 1996).

The questions of accountability, massive expenditures on the part of states for higher education, and the interacting principles of productivity, tenure (often translated as job security), and academic freedom, however, have the potential to rive the academy, perhaps forever. As Layzell notes in chapter 1, in part, higher education's problems are related to the public perception that the reward structure for faculty (including tenure) is at variance with what the public believes that IHEs should be doing (undergraduate education and service). It is also clearly the case that the public's perception is that faculty have permanent job security in a nation often dismayed, shocked and reeling from layoffs and permanent downsizings in the corporate world. The exceptional and highly productive worker today, including corporate America's more senior (and therefore experienced) workforce, can no longer expect that he or she will stay to retirement with the same firm; indeed, it is often those most experienced, those in their most productive years, those most able to recollect and utilize organizational history who are downsized out of a job first. The "joys of tenure," with their presumed "lifetime contracts" (Rosenbaum, 1993), are looked at as creating an academic workforce which is singularly less productive than it might be, and enjoying the fruits of permanent contracts without any effective accountability.

Layzell's contention is that the policy frameworks that have surrounded higher education and the work of the faculty will have to change, radically, as a result of a changing climate of public opinion, economic data, and marketplace concerns. In chapter 2, Tierney attempts to do exactly what Layzell recommends, but seeks to do so within the unique cultural and production frameworks at least two of which have characterized higher education for many centuries, and which Layzell himself outlines. These include "a high level of autonomy . . . asynchronous production . . . [and] the preeminence of the discipline in faculty life." Tierney's proposition for a framework within which to consider academic productivity is rooted in the newest work on the re-creation of community in higher education, such as that of Parker Palmer, in liberal traditions of difference as strength (Tierney, 1993), and in professional traditions of self-governance and self-policing.

Fairweather's chapter in this same volume (chapter 3) takes exactly the opposite stance as Tierney's, but is compatible with Layzell's analyses. His argument is based on the analysis that "the willingness and ability of academic institutions to respond effectively to these challenges is by what Clark . . . calls institutional sagas . . . that help perpetuate organizational culture . . . in part by establishing norms . . . One such norm, the widely held belief that the key to academic reform lies in the collective decisions by faculty and administrators, . . . potentially can thwart attempts by legislators, agencies and public critics to influence faculty work".

Thus, while Tierney believes the impetus for change can be found in academic culture and academic community, Fairweather believes there is little hope for reform to emerge from this locus, precisely because of the nature of academic norms and norming processes, and the power of institutional sagas.

Fairweather's analyses undermine the notion of the "complete professor," the faculty member who is strong in teaching and research, and quite possibly service in addition. In this respect, his work follows the 1976 analyses of Tuckman, who argued that faculty will engage in those activities for which they are most often and most highly rewarded, and that further, the skills that are practiced and honed are those utilized and rewarded, and that the honing of one set of skills (e.g., research) leads often to the languishing of other sets of skills (e.g., teaching or public service).

In chapter 4, Diamond and Adam enter the conversation with another, more recent set of arguments, first widely proposed by the late Ernest Boyer (1990). In *Scholarship Reconsidered,* Boyer dissected four contexts of scholarship—discovery, integration (synthesis), application, and teaching (pp. 15–25)—and suggested that one way to consider the career and productivity of a faculty member might be to look at the various forms of scholarship in which one might engage productively and usefully over a career.

Diamond and Adam echo this more refined and sophisticated understanding of how knowledge is produced, synthesized, and transmitted, suggesting a reward system more finely attuned to the variety and scope of faculty tasks and more sensitively assessed among diverse faculty via evaluation systems and forms developed directly from the emerging understandings.

In chapter 5, Hearn's syntheses of various proposals in higher education for coupling (or uncoupling) faculty salary structures to (or from) scholarly and teaching productivity help those in the conversation comprehend what the benefits and decrements are to various proposals for reward (predominantly, salary) structures in higher education. It is clear from Hearn's discussion that there are no perfect systems for rewarding faculty, few possibilities for avoiding "salary compression," and no one way for all institutions to appropriately reward each individual according to his or her productivity, uniquely. A system more fine-grained, more sensitively attuned to the diverse interests, skills, roles, and strengths of faculty, and more comprehensive in its recognition of the scope of faculty activities (such as the proposal by Diamond and Adam) might ease some of the difficulties with the traditional reward systems reviewed by Hearn. But such a system is also labor-intensive, and requires the kind of profoundly honest community that Tierney envisions as the initial site of reform of academic reward structures. While it is not impossible to realize this kind of academic community, it is easier to imagine its being created first in the confines of a small, liberal arts college, rather than in large, Research I multiversities, where the competition for resources, multiple missions, loose coupling of academic units, and standards for rewards which differ among and between colleges and schools make the establishment of community problematic.

In short, some chapters reinforce other chapters, while others contradict. In the final analysis, it is unimportant whether the chapter authors agree with one another. Indeed, it is probably healthy they do not, because to agree wholly would be to indicate erroneously that the issues of tenure and academic productivity measures are simple conundrums, solvable simply by reading this book. Nothing could be farther from the truth. The structures in place now were created over considerable time, and with considerable cost to individuals and institutions (and, some would say, to students). Further, the issues emerged, and remain problematic, within a culture that is undergoing profound self-examination, especially with respect to who its young people are, what education they should receive, and where those same young adults will fit given a rapid transformation of economic structures and the creation of a global economy.

Nevertheless, each of the chapters is both an entryway and a crowbar. They are places to enter the conversation, and tools to prise open a set of practices that may need to be transformed to reflect new ways of doing creative and scientific work, and new images of what higher education's form should be in the future. Each reflects, too, a set of concerns about how we view tenure and academic productivity. It remains to be seen which views will prevail.

WHAT ELSE NEEDS TO BE INCLUDED IN THE CONVERSATION?

For the moment, however, there are pieces of the conversation that have not yet been enjoined. Although the previous chapters provide excellent fodder for entering the debates surrounding tenure and productivity, there are three issues left still unexplored. First, it is unclear whether the public is sufficiently knowledgeable about the contributions of higher education to basic and applied research, including such research as that which creates new jobs, new technologies, and entirely new industries, to make an informed judgment regarding whether the *primary* purpose of higher education is undergraduate education and public service.

In part, this is what presidents and board members mean when they treat public criticism of IHEs as a public relations problem. Such higher education administrators and spokespersons are not merely acting naive, nor may they be lightly accused of hiding their heads in the sand, ostrichlike. They intuitively understand both sides of the problem: the complexity of tasks and roles that modern universities undertake, some of which are nearly invisible to John Q. Public, and some of which are poorly understood and/or misperceived, and the inability of any spokesperson to represent adequately the complexity involved in modern universities (especially very large, public research universities). Case in point, not even many faculty completely understand the changes that have been wrought on campuses in the past 25 to 50 years. Senior faculty hired a quarter-century ago sometimes express great confusion, exasperation, and anxiety regarding how their own institutions have changed, and how the ground rules have changed.

How are these changes to be explained to parents and other stakeholders?

Second, it is unclear whether the current debates throughout the scholarly and administrative literature, and the media, with their focus on productivity and economic productivity functions, recognize that the qualitative content of faculty work probably cannot and will never be quantifiable. By qualitative content, I mean a complex set of transactions that extend from gifted undergraduate teaching which opens students to the possibilities of a variety of fields of study to inspired mentoring of graduate students through a scientific dissertation. Included in that range of non quantifiable transactions would be student academic advising of all kinds; fostering developmental and maturational change in students; providing mature and stable advisorship to a variety of student organizations, including those which have as their focus the training for postgraduate leadership roles and community service volunteering; consultations about job opportunities and potential careers; faculty governance and curricular decision making; advising various governmental and corporate organizations regarding arenas of faculty expertise; providing (largely unpaid) speakers for service organizations, high school graduations, and other community ceremonial events; creating scientific exchanges around new findings (e.g., medicine), new technologies (e.g., the creation of new food plants for impoverished areas of the world), or new social science understandings (e.g., providing expert testimony to Congress on public policy); and the like. It is also the case that many aspects of classroom teaching embody nonquantifiable productions; an example would be enlarged understandings of undergraduates of their physical, social, and aesthetic worlds, understandings which might not be evident on outcomes assessments until many years after graduation.

While the foregoing argument shares some characteristics with the traditionally defensive academic posture of "trust me/us we know what we're doing," nevertheless the argument has extensive grounding in studies of student change and student development since the Bennington studies of the early part of the twentieth century, and therefore cannot be dismissed readily.

Third, the relationships between faculty tenure, productivity and academic freedom have not been well explored. Nor are they likely to be when institutions rush to write post-tenure review policies (Tierney, 1997), or to abolish tenure altogether.

Tenure was never intended to be a reward per se; and yet it is treated by outsiders to the academy as a perquisite that guarantees permanent job security, whatever the productivity level. Tenure and its historic rationale have never been understood by those not engaged in scholarly pursuits or teaching, and yet it is critical to unfettered exploration of knowledge boundaries, and to countercultural work, whether in the hard sciences or in the arts, literature, or the social sciences.

It is unclear to some faculty, especially those who are doing work that is occasionally unpopular to those in the mainstream of the discipline, whether academic freedom will be adequately protected without tenure. While it is argued that academic freedom is guaranteed by a variety of other measures, it is by no means clear that "other measures" will be adequate (the very reason tenure was created historically). Nor do those of us who have observed firsthand the politics of knowledge creation have confidence that intellectual renegades and counterdisciplinary researchers will find adequate protections from the high-handed norming of mainstream disciplinary practitioners. Consequently, academic freedom's interaction with tenure, productivity, and reward systems discussions cannot be lightly dismissed.

The issues above do not exhaust the possibilities for complex dialogue around tenure, productivity, and rewards, but they do indicate where major public and intrauniversity conflicts might lie. And they suggest that a profession must join the conversation posthaste.

REFERENCES

Bloom, Allan. (1987). The closing of the American mind: How higher education has filed democracy and impoverished the souls of today's students. New York: Simon and Shuster.

Boyer, Ernest L. (1990). Scholarship reconsidered: Priorities of the professoriate. Princeton, NJ: Carnegie Foundation for the Advancement of Teaching.

Bromwich, David. (1992). Politics by other means: Higher education and group thinking. New Haven, CT: Yale University Press.

D'Souza, Dinesh. (1991). Illiberal education: The politics of race and sex on campus. New York: Free Press.

Fairweather, James S. (1996). Faculty work and public trust: Restoring the value of teaching and public service in American academic life. Boston: Allyn and Bacon.

Graff, Gerald. (1992). Beyond the culture wars: How teaching the conflicts can revitalize American education. New York: Norton.

Gross, Paul R., and Levitt, Norman. (1992). Higher superstition: The academic left and its quarrels with science. Baltimore, MD: Johns Hopkins University Press.

Lucas, Christopher J. (1996). Crisis in the academy: Re-thinking higher education in America. New York: St. Martin's Press.

Menand, Louis (Ed.). (1996). The future of academic freedom. Chicago: University of Chicago Press.

Rosenbaum, David E. (1993, December 12). Amid joblessness, the joys of tenure. The New York Times, p.19.

Tierney, William G. (1993). Building communities of difference: Higher education in the twenty—first century. Westport, CT: Bergin and Garvey.

————. (1997, May–June). Academic community and post-tenure review. Academe, 83(3), 23–25.

Tuckman, Howard P. (1976). Publication, teaching, and the academic reward structure. Lexington, MA: Lexington Books.

Index